UPGRADE YOUR LIFE

UPGRADE YOUR LIFE

How to take back control and achieve your goals

PAT DIVILLY

CAPSTONE

This edition first published 2017
© 2017 Pat Divilly

Registered office
John Wiley and Sons Ltd, The Atrium, Southern Gate, Chichester, West Sussex, PO19 8SQ, United Kingdom

For details of our global editorial offices, for customer services and for information about how to apply for permission to reuse the copyright material in this book please see our website at www.wiley.com.

Wiley publishes in a variety of print and electronic formats and by print-on-demand. Some material included with standard print versions of this book may not be included in e-books or in print-on-demand. If this book refers to media such as a CD or DVD that is not included in the version you purchased, you may download this material at http://booksupport.wiley.com. For more information about Wiley products, visit www.wiley.com.

Designations used by companies to distinguish their products are often claimed as trademarks. All brand names and product names used in this book and on its cover are trade names, service marks, trademarks or registered trademarks of their respective owners. The publisher and the book are not associated with any product or vendor mentioned in this book. None of the companies referenced within the book have endorsed the book.

Limit of Liability/Disclaimer of Warranty: While the publisher and author have used their best efforts in preparing this book, they make no representations or warranties with the respect to the accuracy or completeness of the contents of this book and specifically disclaim any implied warranties of merchantability or fitness for a particular purpose. It is sold on the understanding that the publisher is not engaged in rendering professional services and neither the publisher nor the author shall be liable for damages arising herefrom. If professional advice or other expert assistance is required, the services of a competent professional should be sought.

Library of Congress Cataloging-in-Publication Data

Names: Divilly, Pat, author.
Title: Upgrade your life : how to take back control and achieve your goals / Pat Divilly.
Description: Chichester, United Kingdom : John Wiley & Sons, 2017. | Includes
    index.
Identifiers: LCCN 2016027832| ISBN 9780857087263 (pbk.) | ISBN 9780857087256
    (epub)
Subjects: LCSH: Goal (Psychology) | Change (Psychology) | Success.
Classification: LCC BF505.G6 D58 2017 | DDC 650.1–dc23 LC record available at https://lccn.loc
    .gov/2016027832

A catalogue record for this book is available from the British Library

ISBN 978-0-857-08726-3 (paperback) ISBN 978-0-857-08710-2 (ebk)
ISBN 978-0-857-08725-6 (ebk)

Cover design: Wiley
Illustrations by Janice Barrett

10 9 8 7 6 5 4 3 2 1

Set in 10/13pt Myriad Pro by Thomson Digital, Noida, India
Printed in Great Britain by TJ International Ltd, Padstow, Cornwall, UK

Dedicated to my parents who taught me the value of working hard, living simply and the importance of being kind to anyone who crosses my path. For this and so much more, I am thankful and grateful I get to be your son.

CONTENTS

SET YOUR INTENTION

'Success is reserved for the people who never give up.'

Pat Divilly

You have picked up this book for a reason, and I have no doubt you'll get a lot from it and the exercises within it, but as you'll find out later in the book, you're much more likely to get what you want when you are specific on your goals. So, before you read any further, I would like you to set your intention on what exactly it is you want to achieve by reading *Upgrade Your Life*. Rather than looking at this book as just another big bulk of information or another form of entertainment, I want you to look at it as the spark that will fuel your new way of living. Before going even a page further, ask yourself the following questions: What kind of person do you want to become? What kind of life do you want to live? What career do you want? What adventures do you want to have and enjoy?

Whatever it is, decide on it now and write it below. Once you have employed the rituals outlined in this book for the timeframe I recommend, you will one day be able to look back on these goals and realize you have achieved them!

Your Name Here: _____

Set Your Intention for the Book:

IT'S TIME FOR AN UPGRADE!

Before you can change the marketplace or people's attitudes, you must first change what's going on between your ears. When I wrote *Upgrade Your Life*, I did so with some very strong intentions in mind. I want to provide you with a structured plan that will enable you to achieve your goals in life and business, but more importantly, I want to change your perspective.

This isn't a book filled with positive affirmations, nor is it a book that will dole out the same ol' information you've read in many a self-improvement book before. I regularly give motivational seminars, and each one has been a massive success with every seat selling out in no time. My seminars were so successful because the information I provided to those in attendance actually worked. It was an equal blend of theory with action. I have now taken my formula for success and put it into this book for you to use. The exercises and ideas in this book helped me go from working in a pizza restaurant to having my own fitness business with 10,000 clients all over the world. It helped my 50-year-old client Tommy Palmer go from being unhappy and over-weight to qualifying as a personal trainer; it has helped 34-year-old Gill go from being unhappy with her life to taking charge and opening two now hugely successful restaurants. You will read more about Tommy's and Gill's stories later on in the book.

We upgrade our cars, our computers, and our phones, but what about our rituals, our mind-sets, and our ways of thinking? Trust me, when you start to dream creatively and take action, you discover a whole new perspective of how great things could be. There's any amount of self-help books out there – it's an industry in itself – but what I want to introduce in this book is a practical approach to this. It's a combination of my own experience and lessons learned from my own mentors.

Of all the lessons and rituals outlined in this book, improving the way in which you speak to yourself is ultimately the most important one of all in this process. Willpower with the success journal will only get you so far. To enjoy sustainable change over time, you will need to improve your internal dialogue as this will become the most pivotal factor. I'm sure this is something you have read before, especially if you're a reader of self-development books. Now is the time you need to apply this advice.

My Story

'Pat, the European Director of Facebook phoned, and he wants you to call him back.' That was the message waiting for me when I arrived in the gym one morning back in 2014. I thought it was a joke. Turns out it wasn't! Ciarán Quilty, the European Director for Facebook, really did want to speak with me, and the shock didn't end there either. Ciarán told me that the Facebook team had been sharing the 'Pat Divilly Fitness' story at conferences around the world and now they wanted me to join a small group of fellow entrepreneurs at the Facebook HQ in Dublin for a special event. This wasn't a usual 'get together', something I realized when Ciarán told me that the company's Chief Operational Officer, Sheryl Sandberg, was going to be in attendance. The event was to be the first Facebook Small Business Council, so they wanted to bring together a small handful of business owners who were using the platform effectively.

We were all from very different industries, but with Facebook as our primary means of publicity.

On the morning of the event, I headed up to Dublin, not so much with butterflies in my stomach, more like hyperactive bats! Sheryl Sandberg is an icon and meeting her in person was just too surreal to comprehend.

The event itself was exclusive in size but massively significant in terms of impact. The world's press were also in attendance. As Sheryl walked into the room, she looked at the crowd, smiled, and asked, 'Is Pat here?' She spotted me in the front row where I was sitting, and to my shock added, 'Does everyone know Pat's story? Would you like to tell your story, Pat, or will I?'

I let her do the honours.

To this day, I still find it hard to believe!

I mean, Sheryl Sandberg . . . standing in front of a room full of people . . . telling them the story of how I, a boy from Barna, had used Facebook to grow my fitness brand from five clients to 5,000. I honestly thought it couldn't get any better than that!

I was wrong!

Fast forward two years and I was on Necker Island hanging out with Richard Branson. A photo of me with Branson appeared in the local newspapers in my home city. In it, I'm dressed as Bowie – face paint and all – while Branson himself is dressed in a similarly garish costume. I should point out here that he had thrown a fancy dress party, hence the dress code! A week later I was flying out to Nepal, where I had been invited to give a talk on entrepreneurship.

Not half-bad for a guy who failed in his first foray into the fitness business. Experiences such as meeting Sheryl Sandberg and Richard Branson only furthered my belief that if I had the courage to dream and the willingness to do the work consistently, anything was possible.

I was absorbed in the whole self-improvement genre as a teenager but I didn't apply the information I was reading, which was why I wasn't enjoying results back then. That's a big problem with these types of books. Application is crucial but it's the one thing most people fail to do.

I'm a student of self-development and as nerdy as it might seem, I spend a lot of my free time attending seminars all over the world. Often I will leave a full-day seminar after just an hour because I will have acquired the one piece of information I need to take action on an idea. I believe if we took action on 10% of what we already know, we could be incredibly successful. Most of us have the information we need to do things like lose weight, make money, enjoy better relationships, etc. Where we fall is in the application of this information.

Self-development books will either raise your self-esteem or your shelf-esteem. So are you buying them to have a more impressive book shelf or are you buying them because you actually want to improve your life in ways you never thought possible? Unlike other books, *Upgrade Your Life* will force you to apply everything you learn within these pages. The success journal at the end of the book will further help you turn my advice into life-changing habits. While I often reference business owners and entrepreneurs throughout the book, it is certainly not limited to those who are self-employed. In fact, the *Upgrade Your Life* rituals can be implemented right across the board.

Most books get read and left on the shelf. I want you to scribble all over this one. I have created exercises I want you to fill out, and left spaces for notes I want you to make. It's important that you do these. Don't skim over them. They are there for a reason. As kids in school, we drew, we wrote, our imaginations ran free. We spent as much time dreaming with our eyes open as we did with them closed. Let's get back to that creative process. If you don't want to write on the book itself, then get yourself a notebook and complete the exercises in that, so that you can repeat this routine for future goals in different areas of your life.

Remember, everything comes down to thoughts, words, and actions, especially success. When you write something on paper, it becomes a little more real, when you verbalize it, the idea starts to grow because you talk it into existence. When you take action, however, that's when you start to see the biggest change. The success journal will help you with those three crucial elements.

The success rituals, guidelines, and principles I share with you in this book are to be carried out for six weeks straight. If you heed my advice and implement them for those 42 days, then there is no doubt about it – your life will change. You might be wondering why six weeks? I chose six weeks because I know from my own experience that you will witness tangible results in that timeframe.

None of these rituals will work in isolation, however. It's not enough to carry out just one guideline, you must implement them all over the six-week period. Don't worry, the success journal at the end will help keep you on track.

As you make your way through *Upgrade Your Life*, you will understand that the key to accomplishment is through a combination of consistency and the compound effect (i.e. small steps carried out on a daily basis over a consistent period of time). Once you make these rituals a non-negotiable part of your daily routine, you will see one result: success. Everything becomes a lot easier. You become more productive, your relationships are better, your health improves, you are more focused, more grounded, not to mention less stressed. And those are just some of the side effects!

People are not taking time to think about what they want. If you don't think about what you want, then you just fall into receiving whatever is left. *Upgrade Your Life* will not only help you establish what you want from your life, it will radically change and improve your mind-set so you are best placed to achieve your goal.

By the time you have finished this book, you will be a different person. In the meantime, start preparing yourself for a big change and above all, don't be afraid to think big! Your ideas are free, your thoughts are free, you have nothing to lose and an amazing life to gain.

CHAPTER 1

THE RECIPE FOR SUCCESS

'The mind is a powerful force. It can enslave us or empower us. It can plunge us into the depths of misery or take you to heights of ecstasy. Learn to use it wisely.'
— David Cuschieri, author

The one thing I always try to help people understand is that there's a recipe for everything. Wealth, weight loss, success, a cake . . . everything! If you think the great success stories and entrepreneurial billionaires of our age were all heirs and rich kids who were given lucky breaks by the dozen, then think again. Some of them had very little; some of them had absolutely nothing at all, but here's the thing. None of them waited until they had everything or until 'the time was right'. They simply made the best of what they had, and now as a result they have the best of everything. The secrets of their success lie in their attitude and self-belief, not money or circumstances. They set their sights on what they wanted, followed the recipe, and simply didn't give up.

There's a misconception out there that you need to have a full plan in place before you can take action, but in my experience all you really have to do is take one step forward. Just one.

When I talk about this at my personal development seminars, I always liken the journey to walking a spiral staircase. It's only as you progress further that the steps start to unfold. Clichéd? Perhaps, but it's true. You are never going to see 10 steps ahead but you will always see the next one, so take it regardless of how small it may be. I genuinely believe this is what deters people from taking the big leap into entrepreneurship. It is human nature to want to assume full control and protect yourself from oncoming dangers, so naturally some people are going to feel uncomfortable with only being able to see one step ahead at any given time. Don't let this discomfort deter you.

In 2014, I was running a gym in the west of Ireland, and even though we were considered small fish in the fitness industry, myself and a number of others still managed to bring the world's biggest team to an adventure race in Dublin and raise €165,000 in the process. It all started off as an idea, a crazy idea in fact, and one I put out there with no clue as to how we would go about achieving it. We just set the intention and made it public. After we took that first step, things started to happen and take shape. If we had worried about the end result before we had even begun, it would never have happened. If we had allowed ourselves to be deterred by the natural discomfort that comes with embarking on such a big ambition, we would still be sitting around making plans in an attempt to cover every conceivable thing that could go wrong. Instead we decided on a goal, put it out there, and took the first step to get us started.

Similarly, on a recent trip to Nepal I met with a man who wanted to build a hospital for children with cancer. His own son had battled the disease, and to access the necessary treatment, they'd had to travel back and forth to India. He wanted to build a hospital in Nepal so other people wouldn't have to travel, but felt completely overwhelmed. He kept looking at the massive scale of the project rather than the first step, and consequently felt unsure of where to begin. I told him his first step would be to phone the hospital in India and speak to a doctor or a consultant there about his plans. Doing this would then lead him to his next step. I genuinely have no doubt he will get there in the end, but it all has to start with that first step, otherwise it will never happen at all.

I firmly stand by the motto I introduced you to in the introduction, 'when you dream more creatively, and more importantly when you act on it, you start to discover a whole new perspective of how great life could be'.

Some people never even get as far as the 'dream big' stage. Those that do very often don't take the necessary steps forward. Then there are those that have convinced themselves they *can't* move forward because of circumstances. If you fall into this category, then here's what you need to realize. It doesn't matter how down-on-your-luck you are right now, you're in a position to transform your life if you are willing to follow those who have done so before you.

The highest achievers in every industry have at some point taken their biggest adversity or their lowest low point and used it as fuel to turn their lives around. No one succeeds without hitting the proverbial wall, and I guarantee you that almost everyone on the Sunday Times rich list has seen rock bottom at least once. The one thing that differentiated them from the majority, however, was their reaction to the situation. You cannot discount the impact of that factor in their subsequent success.

My own key low point – the one that subsequently led to me starting a fitness business – occurred on Christmas Eve, 2011. After being let go from a commercial gym, I launched a business as a personal trainer offering one-to-one sessions, but I really struggled to make ends meet. I borrowed money for the rent, and even took on a second job of working in a clothes shops to try to keep myself financially afloat. Meanwhile on social media, I was portraying an image that in no way reflected the real situation. I was just too proud and too stubborn to admit that things weren't going that well for me.

Eventually, however, I had to admit defeat and move home. I was so strapped for cash, I had to borrow the bus fare from my dad. What hurt me most of all was the fact that I couldn't afford to even buy my mum a gift for her birthday. Instead all I could do was give her a card with the promise that I would take her to dinner once things picked up for me. That was my rock bottom, undoubtedly.

In the months that followed, my sense of worthlessness caused me to sink into a depression. I had banked on Dublin being a success, and when that didn't happen, I was at a complete loss over what to do next. I felt like I was back at square one. I got myself a part-time job in Fat Freddy's Pizza Restaurant in Galway City. On my days off, I would walk up and down Silver Strand Beach for hours on end just trying to come up with some break-through business idea or revelation. At the time, I was playing the blame game, pointing the finger at everyone and everything apart from myself. I blamed the cheap rates offered by commercial gyms, the impact of the recession, and everything in between.

During one of my beach walks, back in March/April of 2012, it occurred to me that there were plenty of trainers out there making a perfectly good living from the fitness industry in spite of the recession and the rates offered by the fitness chains. Yes, the country was in a bad recession at the time and money was certainly tight for everyone, but I figured if other guys were making money from the fitness business then there must be a way. Following this realization, I decided to contact a few personal trainers in the UK. These were guys I had been following on social media and who looked like they were doing really well in business, so I asked them if they could give me some advice on how I could get started. My way clearly wasn't working so it made sense to speak to those who were doing well.

I received a reply from a trainer in Cardiff called Mark Tregilgas who at the time was enjoying great success with his fitness camp. In his response, he gave me the encouragement I needed to start again in the form of a few tips to help me on my way. I took on board everything he said and sat down to create a plan. For a long time I told myself that I would start the fitness class on my local beach in Barna *but only when* 20 people signed up. Eventually I just decided to set a date and regardless of whether two people signed up or 200, I would train them as best as I possibly could.

Once the date was set, I had to get the word out there and advertise. As I didn't have a budget – shoestring or otherwise – both newspaper and radio ads were out of the question, so I figured the next best thing would be flyers. I went into Galway City and ordered a print run of 5,000. They were still hot off the printing press when I dropped them all over the city, leaving them anywhere I thought my target audience would see them.

Five people turned up at my very first session on that day in May 2012. Most trainers would have packed it in after that but for me it was a starting point. By the second month, I was training 20 people, and by the third, I was up to 100. I felt completely renewed; my sense of ambition and purpose were both back in full force. In hindsight, I can honestly say that my low point made me a better trainer. Having experienced such a hard time on a personal level made me realize that everyone was struggling with something. It made me more determined to make my fitness class a place where people could escape their daily stresses and forget about whatever was bothering them. Overall, my strategy was simple – I would try to make my class the best part of their day.

Those early days of the business were far from easy. I didn't have a car so instead I would cycle 30 minutes from my workplace in the city to the beach in Barna where I would hold my class. On a fine day, cycling that coast road out to Barna is idyllic, but in the pouring rain, it's probably the fastest route to pneumonia! Sometimes I would make this journey three or four times a day. Later, as the demand for classes grew, I would end up cycling all around the city to four different locations where the classes were taking place. Yes, it was difficult, but it wasn't about comfort or convenience, it was about progress, and I was willing to do whatever it took to make my business even just 1% better each day.

When I wasn't teaching the classes, I was writing articles, recording podcasts, and trying to grow my social media pages.

This only happened after I realized that the way to become successful in business was to add value to what I was offering, something I will cover later in the book. This is the only way anyone can become outrageously successful in business. During the very early days, however, I was doing the opposite. I was trying to make the money *before* I gave the value. I was asking people to buy my products and pay for my services before I had proved my worth. I had the attitude that if someone wasn't paying me then I wouldn't give away my knowledge or skills. I see now that it should have been the other way around. I should have been giving away the good quality content for free in order to show people what I was capable of. I have shared my own story so many times that my friends and family could probably do a good job reciting it word for word themselves, but I don't tell it for me. It's not about me anymore. I have already lived that part of my life. My hope is that the story will help inspire others.

The thing you need to know about me is that I grew up on a diet of personal development books. My dad's book shelves were filled with the teachings of the great self-improvement gurus and masters of popular psychology. Napoleon Hill's *Think and Grow Rich* was one of the first books I ever read, followed by Dale Carnegie's *How to Win Friends & Influence People*. Those two books had such a profound impact on me. I used to rave about them at school until one day a friend of mine said to me, 'Well if they're that good, why read so many of them? Should you not read just one and be able to see results from that?'

He was right. The reason I never saw results was because I was reading the material but not applying it. After I hit my low point I returned to my dad's book shelf and started reading again, only this time, I applied action. Within the 12 months that followed my first fitness class on the beach, I had opened a fitness studio in Barna and signed my first book deal. Television work was plentiful, and my online following was over 100,000. My business was thriving and going from strength to strength; I was constantly on the go. The demand for my services was phenomenal, which is why it probably came as a big surprise to many when, in 2015, I made the decision to sell the gym. Don't get me wrong, I'm still very much in the fitness business, I just don't run the gym any more. I will explain in the next chapter what influenced my decision to sell but I can say with my hand on my heart that it was the best thing I ever did. Following the sale, I started implementing certain rituals – all of which are outlined in this book – and they have improved my life and career so much.

This year so far, I have travelled around America, Europe, Africa, Nepal, and Dubai. A huge ambition of mine was also realized when I took to the stage to present a TEDx talk. Without a doubt, however, the number one highlight of my year – and definitely one of the greatest highlights of my life – was meeting one of my idols, Richard Branson, at his home on Necker Island.

I was part of a mastermind group of 25 people that had the amazing opportunity to travel to Necker and hang out with Branson. 'Surreal' doesn't even come close to how it felt.

Funnily enough, the weekend prior to the trip, I watched Branson doing an interview on *The Late Late Show*. I have to say Branson came across exactly as you would expect. The man you see on television is the man you meet in person. There's no bullshit with him. He's real and has never made any apology for it. The day we met him, he seemed a little bit dejected. He later explained that his business baby, Virgin Airlines, had been sold for around a billion dollars the day before we arrived. He had been against the sale, but as he only owned 20% of the company, there was nothing he could do to stop the sale from going ahead. He even said at one point that it was the 'worst billion dollar cheque' he had received.

During the Q&A, he willingly answered a barrage of questions, while also speaking a great deal about his space travel ambitions. The big thing I took from Necker was the huge scope of possibility that's open to us all. When you travel to an inspiring environment like Necker, especially in the company of individuals who each have an Olympian level of ambition, you're presented with a whole new realm of thinking. It broadens your perspective of what's possible in life and really motivates you to achieve it.

I love the quote, '*Small minds discuss people, average minds discuss events, great minds discuss ideas.*' Our whole trip was spent discussing ideas. There were 25 people on that trip and every single person was doing something amazing with their life. They were all working towards their goals. The people you surround yourself with really do have an impact on how you think and while I have always been aware of that fact, this trip 100% re-enforced it even more. Even just being in the company of someone like Richard Branson, whose thinking has no limitations, rubs off and you leave there feeling fired up and bursting with ideas.

I learned a lot from the brief time I spent on Necker, but one thing stands out. Regardless of your current circumstances, it pays to think big.

Business and life lessons from a billionaire

- When it comes to networking or developing your team, forget the stiff business meetings. Look at ways in which you can make things fun. When we were on the island, Branson threw a fancy dress party for the group and even arrived in full costume too. He makes a point of incorporating fun into everything he does, and this has no doubt contributed to the success of his business.
- I speak more about this later in the book when I talk about the benefits of mastermind groups, but if you want to succeed, then the best way in which to do so is to surround yourself with others who are equally as passionate about success as you are.
- Possibilities really are endless. From big dreams come big ideas and from those come big prospects. You just need to think BIG!
- Nice guys exist in business. You don't have to play Mr Nasty to get to the top. Richard Branson is testament to this.

  Don't confuse risk-taking with recklessness. It pays to take risks, to go with your gut, but risk-taking in business should also have a strong element of calculation behind it.

Upgrading My Life: Jac Keady (client)

When I met Pat, I was a stay-at-home mum and my redundancy money had run out. I faced the prospect of returning to a boring 9–5 job and leaving my longed-for baby in someone else's care. I genuinely believed my life was mapped out for me and I had to settle for an average life with a fortnight's holiday once a year to keep me going.

Pat inspired me to believe that anything is possible, so based on my passion for cooking, I started my own Paleo food company. The sense of achievement seeing your products on supermarket shelves is immense and I will forever be grateful to Pat for teaching me to realize anything is possible and the only limitations we have are in our head. I only wish more people could discover the potential that lies dormant inside them and not waiting until they're richer, stronger or slimmer to be happy, but instead, choose to be happy right now.

CHAPTER 2

THE UPGRADE

'It is important to be willing to make mistakes. The worst thing that can happen is you become memorable.'
— Sara Blakely, Spanx entrepreneur

What is success?

'Kill him, Badger, kill him!'

Those were the words 15-year-old British boxer Luke Campbell heard just as he was about to step into the boxing ring for his first ever international match for England. He didn't know anything about his opponent other than the fact that he was Scottish . . . and presumably called Badger if the side line roars of the teenager's mother were anything to go by. Despite the distraction of a one-woman murder chorus, Luke went on to win that match 16 points to 8. Fast forward 13 years and he is the proud owner of an Olympic gold medal and a stateside career in a sport he loves. For him, the ultimate success was taking home the Olympic gold. He viewed every training session and every win as a step closer to success because he knew exactly what he was working towards.

The following piece of advice is one I cannot stress often enough. You *need* to establish what success would look like to you. The stereotypical image of success would probably involve taking ownership of things like a Lamborghini, a Rolex, wall-to-wall shelves of Louboutins, etc, but what would success look like *to you*? What would make you feel like you have achieved success? Maybe it's being able to bring your family on holiday, maybe it's owning the aforementioned Lambo?

Those looking in at my life might presume my ultimate successes were experiences such as meeting Facebook COO Sheryl Sandberg and hearing her tell my story to the conference room or visiting Necker Island and meeting Richard Branson. Though I enjoyed those experiences immensely, some of my biggest successes, to me, were in fact owning a business that enabled me to travel quite a bit; having enough money to provide for my family, and being able to take my little brother out for lunch. Four years ago, I couldn't afford to buy my mum a gift for her birthday so now I equate success with being able to do things like treating her to dinner whenever I wish or being able to buy her a beautiful present for absolutely no reason whatsoever.

Success to me is waking up in the morning with good energy, having great relationships with my family, and being able to enjoy two holidays a year. Success is loving what I do for a living. In a world where so many people hate their jobs, live for the weekend, and dread the arrival of Monday, I most definitely consider it a form of success to actually *want* to go to work in the morning.

For a lot of people, success is often defined by what they see on either social or mainstream media but if you don't think about what success would look like to you personally then I don't think you can ever achieve it, nor will you be content with anything you have achieved.

I remember reading a quote by the author Tim Tweedie. It was called *What Does It Mean to Succeed* and every word of it struck a chord with me. Read it slowly and let it sink in.

> *Most people see success as being rich and famous or powerful and influential. Others see it as being at the top of their profession and*

standing out from the rest. The wise see success in a more personal way; they see it as achieving the goals they have set for themselves, and then feeling pride and satisfaction in their accomplishments. The success is felt in the heart, not measured by money or power. So be true to yourself and achieve the goals you set. For success is reaching those goals and feeling proud of what you have accomplished.

This is not to say that fame and fortune don't often follow, but I really do believe that they are a by-product of truly doing what you love and doing it to a high degree of success. People like Richard Branson and Elon Musk became famous and wealthy but not because they chased fame and wealth. Their profile and financial ranking both came about because they added value to the marketplace and worked insanely hard at something they loved. People who chase fame and fortune for the sake of fame and fortune will often find themselves left unfulfilled. You see this regularly with child stars who as adults turn to drink and drugs even though they have the level of wealth and profile that most people dream of. They lack that feeling of fulfilment most likely because they never had the opportunity to define their own vision of personal success. Their career in show business was decided for them and it may not have been one they would have chosen had they been older and the decision theirs to make.

Establishing what success is to you

There's passive learning and then there's active learning. Passive learning is where one sits back and waits for the answers to fall onto one's lap, but here's the thing about passive learners. They never get very far because they're missing the one element required for success: action.

As this book is all about active learning, you are going to take action starting right now. The purpose of the exercise you're about to complete is to help you establish a clear vision of success.

Sit down, turn off your phone, and really focus your thinking. If it helps, spur on the creative process with a cup of coffee. You might find yourself surprised by some of the answers that pop up when you start to think things through.

Once you have given it some thought, write down the top 10 things that would equate to success for you in your business as well as your personal life.

This exercise is so important. I can tell you from experience that achieving a goal you have dreamed of for years, only to realize it's not what you expected, is the emptiest feeling in the world. True success is feeling fulfilled upon reaching your goal.

'Success without fulfillment is the ultimate failure.'
Tony Robbins, self-help author

Core values

Once you have defined your version of success, it is important that you establish your core values. I realized the importance of core values two years ago when I hit a significant low point. I say 'significant' because it was the catalyst I needed to help instigate a change in my professional life.

At the time, things were going really well for me. From an external viewpoint, my life looked perfect. I was running a very successful business and genuinely loving the feeling that came with helping people change their lives. As word of my business spread, I found myself inundated on a daily basis with messages from people eager to become clients. From an outside perspective, I was very successful. Internally, however, I was tormented. I was working myself into the ground and as a consequence, my family and friends rarely ever saw me. Some people thrive on stress – I suppose we all do to some extent – but this level of stress was

UPGRADE YOUR LIFE NOW!

Ten things that equate to success for me.

1.

2.

3.

4.

5.

6.

7.

8.

9.

10.

overwhelming. I had convinced myself that I was taking care of my family, but in reality I wasn't. I was overworked, exhausted, and consequently trapped with guilt.

Around that time, I was reading a lot of books about how to run a successful business, and I noticed that each one spoke about the importance of having core values. Having these core values, they said, would make business decisions easier. If you establish your core values, then you can easily choose the correct endorsements/advertising options, hire the right people, fire the wrong ones, etc.

The core values for my business were 'gratitude', 'belief', 'reciprocity', 'strength', and in particular 'community' because I wanted to bring people together. If someone came to me with a business idea that didn't tie in with those values, then it was easy for me to say no without having to fret over whether or not I had made the right decision.

I figured if it made sense to have core values for my business, then why not have them in place for my personal life? I can't emphasize enough just how incredibly effective they are for helping to shape you into the person you want to become. Funnily enough, few people ever think about this.

As soon as I personally experienced the benefits of having core values in place in my own life, I started helping my seminar attendees establish theirs. Here, I am going to help you establish your core values through the following exercise.

The traits you listed in this exercise should form three of your core values.

The premise of this exercise stems from the idea that when we hold an admiration for a particular person, it's actually the traits within them that we admire. We all have good and bad traits but when you recognize someone as being an individual you look up to or idolize,

UPGRADE YOUR LIFE NOW!

List three people you admire followed by one trait you most admire in each of them.

1.

2.

3.

it's because they've got certain traits you too would like to have. Now that your attention has been directed towards this, you can concentrate on highlighting these traits in your own character. Once you do, you will find yourself morphing into the kind of person you want to be, and, as a result, you will be much happier and content, not to mention more successful.

Remember, our ultimate currency in life is how we treat other people. At the end of your life, it's not going to matter how much money you had in your bank account or what kind of car you drove. What will matter is how you influenced other people and affected their lives for the better.

Remember, your core values should act as a compass to guide you on what you should be doing on a daily basis, as opposed to some sort of strict regimen that must be followed! When you are living outside your core values (or if you have yet not established your core values), that's when you start to feel a little 'off' and the stress starts to gather pace. When you get that feeling, that's when you know you need to revisit your core values.

When I was figuring out my core values, one of the people I listed in the first exercise was my dad. The traits I admired in him were his work ethic, his ability to be a wonderful family man, and the fact that he was always such a genuine person. I, by comparison, was working very hard but I wasn't seeing my family as much as I would have liked. I was genuine but at the same I was doing stuff that I probably didn't enjoy. When I completed the core values task, it made me take stock of things and realize the changes I needed to make.

Another person I listed was my friend Gill Carroll. Gill went from being unemployed to setting up a successful restaurant business. She now runs two restaurants in Galway City and is also heavily involved in charity work. The three traits I admire in her are honesty, her passion for connecting people, and her phenomenal work ethic.

The third person on my list is the Tesla and SpaceX entrepreneur Elon Musk. The traits I most admire in him are his leadership skills, his ability to innovate, and his courage to turn his ideas into a reality regardless of how outlandish they may seem.

Now on to the second core value exercise! For this, I want you to think about the things you would like people to say about you when you're not present. How would you like to be described?

List them!

UPGRADE YOUR LIFE NOW!

List five things you would want people to say about you.

1.

2.

3.

4.

5.

Now you have five more attributes that can help you form more core values. When I carried out this exercise, I wrote that I would like people to say I was loyal, genuine, honest, hardworking, and a family man.

What way do you see yourself? What way are you really? Sometimes we think we are living in a certain way, but deep down we know we are not. I think sometimes we jump into setting huge goals and wanting to change without first forming a true representation of our current situation. Before we can truly change, we must bring awareness to our current situation and tell ourselves the truth. You have to be honest with yourself and say

'I'm not really living that way. It's nice to think I am, but that's a fantasy world and I have to make a change.'

When you live in fantasy land you can't really win, so getting real is the best thing you can do for your journey to success. Step back and realize you are not living the way you want to live. People often shy away from this exercise because it can be hard to admit that you're not the person you have convinced yourself you are.

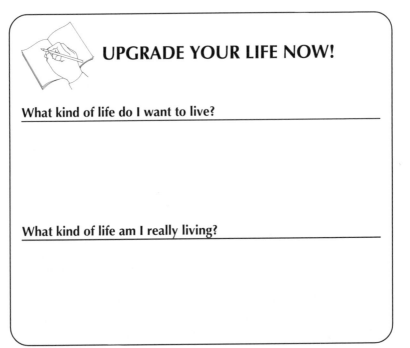

UPGRADE YOUR LIFE NOW!

What kind of life do I want to live?

What kind of life am I really living?

Don't beat yourself up with this exercise. It's not a bad thing that you're not living the life you want to live, or being the kind of business figurehead you want to be. If anything, this realization is a good thing because it means you now have awareness of your situation. When you have awareness of an issue, you can implement the necessary changes.

It's when you lack awareness that you become ignorant of the improvements that need to be made and, as a result, end up coasting through life, never reaching your full potential. So many people harbour a victim mentality all their lives rather than face up to their reality. Remember what I said earlier in the book. In order to change the marketplace and people's attitudes, you need to first change your mind-set.

When I carried out the core values exercise, I won't lie, it was very difficult for me to admit to myself that I wasn't being the good brother, son, or friend that I wanted to be. It was really tough, but becoming aware allowed me to make a big change.

Identifying and implementing my core values made a huge difference to my life both personally and professionally speaking. The moment I realized I was not living in accordance with my core values, I set about making a number of changes. First and foremost, I made more time for the people who were most important to me. My next step was to sell my gym and concentrate instead on expanding my range of online fitness courses, which I still run to this day. I had always told myself I would travel when I retired rich, but a heart-to-heart with a good friend made me realize there was absolutely no sense in waiting. With my business now online, I could work from anywhere in the world, so I packed up and embarked on the most amazing trip. The break relaxed me both physically and mentally. It also enabled me to change my approach to my daily routine – something I will be outlining in greater detail later in the book so you can do it too – and, as a result, my productivity levels soared, my creative thinking process started to generate new project ideas, and my work ethic went from strength to strength without me having to sacrifice time with those who were most important to me.

Had I allowed myself to continue renting a space in fantasy land, I would still be stuck in a very unhappy and highly stressful situation. Establishing your core values requires a level of brutal honesty. Yes, it will hurt, but don't forget a sting is only ever temporary. It's the benefits you reap from this change that will last a lifetime.

The stories you tell yourself

 The stories you tell yourself are either holding you back or pushing you forward.

You talk to yourself more than you do to anyone else in the world, but I would bet good money that most of those internal conversations you're having are pretty negative. You're not alone. People rarely tell themselves empowering things and are slow to feed positive messages to their subconscious.

When I was in school, I used to constantly tell myself I wasn't academic. What I didn't realize at the time, however, is that when you repeatedly tell yourself something you treat as fact, your subconscious immediately looks for the evidence. Your subconscious doesn't want to be wrong so you end up providing yourself with evidence that the stories you repeatedly tell yourself are correct.

For instance, any time I got distracted from my school work, I would convince myself I had attention deficit disorder. When I spoke to my dad about my lack of academic tendencies, he told me that he too had found it hard in school. As a result, I managed to convince myself that it was a genetic thing and out of my control. I know, crazy stuff! I always found a reason to justify my claim that I wasn't academic.

The reality is that if you constantly tell yourself you're not academic, then you're never going to do the things that an academic person would do, so in a way it becomes a self-fulfilling prophecy.

In my seminars I always encourage people to list two empowering stories they could tell themselves. People always struggle with this. It seems to be in our nature to resist self-praise and enforce self-criticism. Let go of that resistance right now and write down two empowering stories you have told yourself followed by two disempowering stories you do tell yourself.

Reframing your stories

My biggest empowering story is: 'If someone else can do something, then there is no reason why I can't do it.'

The disempowering stories I used to tell myself were: 'It's a recession, I can't make money', or 'Irish people can't make a real living from personal training', or the old favourite, 'I'm not academic'.

The way you overcome these disempowering stories is to present yourself with evidence that the story you are telling yourself is not true. In my case, I was telling myself it was a recession and that no one was making money, but plenty of people were making money in the industry I wanted to be in. Straight away I had evidence that my disempowering story held no truth. I also read that more millionaires were made during the depression than at any other time in history. Again, more evidence.

Whenever I heard myself saying I wasn't academic, I simply paused and instead reminded myself that I had sat the state exams and passed each one, which in itself made me somewhat academic. I also reminded myself of my voracious appetite for books, which is one of the traits of an academic person. I basically provided my subconscious with evidence that the negative story was untrue. This is a wonderful way to retrain your brain. Similarly, when my fitness business really started to take off, I began telling myself that it couldn't continue at that pace, that there weren't enough potential clients out there. The reframe for this was: 'Well there's 7 billion people in the world, and the internet opens access to everyone so really I've only scratched the surface.'

UPGRADE YOUR LIFE NOW!

Empowering story 1:

Empowering story 2:

Disempowering story 1:

Disempowering story 2:

I want you to start focusing on how you can reframe those disempowering stories. If you tell yourself something like 'I can't sing', then ask yourself the question: 'Is it that I can't sing, or that I don't sing? Maybe I actually can sing, but just don't have the confidence yet to belt out a tune?'

It's all about becoming conscious of the story that's in your head. If you want a better life, ask yourself better questions. Remove the negative slant from a statement and replace it with a positive question. So, rather than asking yourself 'Why am I so fat?', or 'Why am I poor?' instead ask yourself 'What can I do to improve my health?', or 'How can I improve my financial situation?' Be conscious of that inner dialogue.

How often do you carry forward disempowering stories from your youth or recent years that are not true? These can be so damaging and really limit your perspective. There was one man who attended my seminar and afterwards approached me for a chat. He said he was struggling to find a girlfriend because he was so overweight. The reality was that he had lost 12 stone and was in great shape, but in his head he was still the overweight guy. The story he was telling himself was no longer true yet he had carried it forward from recent years and it stuck with him long after the weight had disappeared.

For this next exercise, I want you to list your two disempowering stories again, followed by the evidence that proves they hold no weight. I also want you to look at how you can reframe each story so that they lose their negative connotation.

It is important that you do this. If you want to be successful in your business and happy in your life, you need to change the manner in which you speak to yourself. Do you think billionaire moguls such as Carl Icahn, Alan Sugar, Richard Branson, Jack Ma, and Len Blavatnik got to where they are in business by constantly criticizing themselves? Not a chance. Success requires an unshakeable self-belief and a good attitude. Start to get into the habit of breaking down the negative self-talk so that you can begin remoulding how you view yourself.

UPGRADE YOUR LIFE NOW!

Disempowering story 1: _____

Evidence it is not true –

Reframe your story –

Disempowering story 2: _____

Evidence it is not true –

Reframe your story –

Upgrade your inner dialogue

Don't forget, your brain listens to absolutely everything you say. You might consider a remark such as 'I'm so stupid' to be a throwaway comment; however, it's anything but. When you self-criticize, you chip away at your character and any progress you have made. Your subconscious hears what you are saying and introduces a whole slew of problems as a result of that inner dialogue.

I know a guy who was on best man duty at his brother's wedding. To say he was dreading the day would be an understatement. He was absolutely terrified by the idea of standing up in front of a crowd and giving the traditional best man speech. He kept talking about how the thought of it made him feel sick with anxiety and how he'd rather do anything else. On the day of the wedding, he broke out in hives as a result of the stress and nerves. His body had physically reacted to his fear of public speaking. What you need to realize is that your brain wants to protect you, so when you tell yourself you are terrified of something, your subconscious reacts to that and does everything in its power to keep you from venturing near 'danger', so to speak.

The language you use when speaking to yourself has a much bigger impact than you realize. For instance, rather than telling himself he was terrified of speaking in front of a crowd, the best man should have started telling himself he was looking forward to the challenge. It's easier said than done, but it would have made a difference.

Successful business people 'reframe and rephrase' all the time. It's second nature to them. They don't beat themselves up over problems and obstacles; they look at them as either challenges to be overcome or as experiences that will help improve their skills. This level of confidence and self-assurance didn't just happen overnight, however. It was developed over time, and trust me, inner dialogue plays a huge role in that process.

I used to be extremely hard on myself, but once I changed the language of my inner dialogue, things started to change for me.

When you start your six-week success journal, I want you to develop a daily habit point of drip-feeding your subconscious with positive language. Build it up more and more as each day goes on. It will be a tough habit to implement at first, particularly if you are quite hard on yourself, but by the end of the six weeks, I guarantee that the positive self-talk will come naturally and you will enjoy a massive change in your confidence levels. The first step is to become aware of the language you are using. Pinpoint the negative words you use on a regular basis and become aware of their presence in your vocabulary.

Example:

Instead of saying 'I am so fat', you should say 'I am working on improving my health every day.' Instead of 'My business failed', say 'I learned so many lessons from my first business.'

Your 'I Am' statement

One of my inspirations, MMA fighter Conor McGregor, has become the poster boy for self-belief. He constantly reminds us that he's the best in the business, and you just know he firmly believes that too. When he says things like 'I am fearless', you don't doubt it for one second. McGregor doesn't care if his critics think he's rubbish, he lets his actions and his successes give them the middle finger. Dwayne 'The Rock' Johnson is the same. He won't hesitate to impress upon you how determined he is to succeed. And of course let's not forget the king of self-belief, Muhammed Ali. His quotes from both inside and outside the boxing ring were the epitome of self-assurance and certainty. This streak of supreme confidence can be found in all massively successful performers, whether it be in business, sport, music, etc. They say what they are, and they believe what they say.

UPGRADE YOUR LIFE NOW!

List the top five negative phrases you most commonly tell yourself followed by the five phrases you will replace them with from now on.

1.

2.

3.

4.

5.

Their inner talk is positive and encouraging, not negative and critical. Yes, they have their despondent moments of doubt, but these 'moments' do not overtake the majority of their thoughts. The most successful figures don't judge themselves by their setbacks and they certainly don't allow those setbacks to define who they are. This is a habit of which most people are guilty, and even though it is one that doesn't serve us in any way, we still fall victim to it time and time again.

'You become what you believe, you are where you are today in your life based on everything you have believed.'

Oprah Winfrey, TV entrepreneur

Your beliefs and what you think about yourself have largely been determined by your environment. Right now, most of what you think you are is as a result of what others have told you. You would be surprised how much this governs a lot of your unconscious behaviour. I completed a course some years back and something the host said always stuck with me: 'Most of us wear identities we didn't choose. We are things people told us we were rather than things we told ourselves we were.'

Your 'I Am' statement is your identity statement. It's a combination of who you think you are and who you want to be. How you speak to yourself governs a lot of how you behave. If you are in the habit of speaking negatively to yourself, then you need to rewire the brain. It's difficult at first but trust me, the more you do it, the more ingrained it becomes.

When I told myself I wasn't academic, I didn't do the things an academic person would do, such as study. If you make yourself believe you are academic or smart, then you will have no issue with the idea of studying. The stories you tell yourself will either help or hinder your progress in both life and business. What you have to do is recognize what's true and what's not.

Remember the guy from the previous section who had lost 12 stone yet still had a story running in his head that he was overweight? This is a prime example of how a story from your past can trickle into your future. Your identity is comprised of what you have told yourself you are up until this point, but here's the key point to remember. Just because you have told yourself something for such a long time, that doesn't make it true. Sometimes we are conditioned to think a certain way because of what our parents would say to us during our formative years. As a kid you think your parents know everything, so everything they tell you becomes a belief.

Where do your beliefs come from?

People born on one side of the world think one way about religion, but people born in a different part of the world think a very different way about it. Another example would be football. People who are born on one side of Manchester will support Man City, yet those born on a different side of Manchester will support Man United. The only reason the two sides think so differently, whether it be about football or religion, is because that's the way they were told to think. It's worth asking yourself if your beliefs are in fact true, or if they were formed as a result of your environment and the people who occupy it. Identify which beliefs are helping you and which ones are hindering you. Are your beliefs making you happy or hateful? Supportive of others or begrudging? Honesty is so crucial here.

 UPGRADE YOUR LIFE NOW!

Your 'I Am' statement.

What do you think you are?

What would you like to be?

Upgrade your identity

When you think about it, you will realize that the contents of your 'I Am' statement have more than likely been taking shape since your childhood. When you are born, you're a clean slate. As you get older and start to understand the world around you, the people in your environment place certain beliefs upon you. Our beliefs shape us, but these beliefs come from the people around us so it's worth taking a look at the absolute truth vs the relative truth. The absolute truth is fact. You walk off a building, you will fall. That's absolute truth. Relative truth, however, is something you have convinced yourself is true.

We're all guilty of attributing certain meanings to incidents that occurred during our younger years and that have since stuck with us into adulthood. Maybe you read aloud in front of the class when you were a teenager and were laughed at? You probably associated that incident with the idea that you are not a good public speaker. That's a relative truth. It's something you convinced yourself of. Here's the good news. Your beliefs are stoppable. You CAN go back and rewrite them. Your childhood will never change, but the meaning you give it most certainly can.

We tend to attach an emotional meaning to different events but the reality is that these events don't carry any meaning at all. It's the meaning *we give them* that causes the negative feelings.

Let's take a general scenario as an example. If someone you know walked past you without saying hello, you would probably jump to the conclusion that they were deliberately ignoring you when in fact they might have been distracted by their own personal issues. It's a reasonable explanation as to why they didn't acknowledge you, yet the chances are you would have immediately assumed that *you* were the reason they were not speaking to you.

Let's say a customer leaves a nasty review on your social media page. Do you take it personally? No. You take a step back and cut through the negative element of the comment so that you can establish what the actual complaint is. Don't pay attention to the negative embellishments, e.g. 'This is the WORST restaurant I have ever had the misfortune of eating in.' Remember, people will always decorate their sentences that bit more when they are angry or upset, and this is especially the case when it comes to writing a negative review, so don't let their choice of words get to you. Once you have worked out what their complaint is, acknowledge it, apologize if necessary, and make amends with the customer so that they leave the conversation with a different perspective of your establishment. These heated exchanges can be tough, and very often they end up feeding the disempowering stories you have already been telling yourself. ('I'm not a good enough business person', etc.) Be mindful of this. Don't give these incidents the power to fuel the relative truths you tell yourself. Instead, focus on the changes you can implement so that there won't be a repeat of the complaint voiced by the previous customer.

Reframe the meaning

Once you stop attaching a meaning to incidents and events, the negative feelings and accompanying stress tend to disappear. Easier said than done, I know, but it's worth taking the time to break the habit over the next six weeks. The next time you find yourself hurt or offended by someone, take a step back and look at it objectively. You are responsible for shaping your identity, no one else. Think it's too late to change who you are? You're wrong!

When it comes to self-belief, few can rival the aforementioned poster boy Conor McGregor. He's known for his bold statements and unshakeable self-belief, but this wasn't an attitude he adopted only when things started to go well in his career. He was like that long before he became a household name and definitely long before the celebration cheers for him sent tremors through Las Vegas. His mind-set is the very reason his career is going so well. He envisioned himself one day being a world champion even back when he was unemployed and on state benefits.

Even today, McGregor will never say that he hopes to win a fight, he will *tell* you with 100% conviction that he is going to win the fight. He's not just talking the talk either. When he sets his mind on a goal, he follows it up with the necessary action.

Notice how it all comes back to action?

I am enough

Deep down, most people think they're not enough. This goes back to childhood. When you're a child, everything is good until you hit age 4 or 5 and you have to start listening to instructions. You go from being able to do what you want and having free reign to suddenly being ordered about.

Maybe your parents were tired after working long hours and often shushed you. Suddenly you started to think 'my voice doesn't matter', when in actual fact it wasn't you at all. Still, you associated a meaning with it that wasn't entirely accurate and it stuck. The more it happened, the more it thwarted your opinion of yourself.

Motivational speaker Marissa Peer has a great technique when it comes to enforcing a necessary self-reminder that you are enough. (I say 'enforcing' because most of us refuse downright to believe we are enough.) Marissa always advises people to write 'I am enough' in lipstick on their mirrors and then leave it there. It's the one place you are guaranteed to see it regularly. When I first heard of this technique, yes I thought it was kind of crazy, but I had nothing to lose by trying it out and deciding for myself whether or not it worked. It's only in recent years that I have become more open to these types of techniques.

Prior to having experienced Marissa's technique for myself, I probably would have regarded it as fluffy nonsense, but I have to say it did make a difference to my mind-set. If you decided to give this technique a try, and I recommend that you do, ensure that you make a conscious effort to read it out to yourself each time you see it, otherwise it loses its effectiveness and becomes something you overlook and eventually forget about.

Before you move on to the next chapter, I want you to take a picture of your 'I Am' statement and save it as your laptop screensaver, phone wallpaper, or pin it somewhere you will see it and heed it daily.

Most of us have inner critics with a lot to say! If yours is pretty yappy, then you can't afford not to do this.

Now, have you completed the success rituals and core value exercises yet? If not, why are you reading on? Go back and complete them.

 ## Chapter 2 Cheat Sheet to Upgrade Your Life

- The disempowering stories you tell yourself hold absolutely no truth.
- Establish your core values. These will act as a compass to guide you on what you should be doing on a daily basis.
- I AM ENOUGH! Write down this mantra, pin it to the fridge/wall/ etc and repeat it whenever you see it.
- When faced with a complaint about your business, step back and cut through the negative element of the comment so that you can establish what the actual complaint is. Then deal with it and move on.
- Become aware of the language you are using and start replacing negative words with ones of a more positive nature.
- You need to establish what success is to you. If you don't become clear on this, you will never get what you want.
- Be an active learner, not a passive one. Passive learners never get very far because they're missing the one element required for success: action.

"

Upgrading My Life: Gill Carroll (client)

'The stronger my mind-set became, the less I feared failure.'

Prior to meeting Pat, I was coasting along in life. I had really lost both my way and my potential. Within 5 months of meeting Pat I quit my job, and opened my first 30-seater cafe a few months later. I have since gone on to open a 130-seater restaurant in the city as well as set up a business supporting female entrepreneurs. I have pushed myself physically in ways I never thought possible. With Pat's encouragement I have also helped raise a lot of money for various charities and continue to do so. But I guess the biggest difference is that I am now truly the person I was meant to be.

I am living my authentic life in line with my core values every day and because of this I can now serve the world I live in, in a much better way.

Before I met Pat, I was living my life in order to keep other people happy; it was not on my own terms, but then I had never asked myself what I wanted. I didn't know who I was and I didn't see potential for myself.

My first big change started with the mind-set. Pat made it fun, he switched me on to reading and re-educating myself. I've learnt more in the past 4 years than I had since school. Once I started to get the right mind-set, the exercise and nutrition kicked in. Getting up early was key as was having a daily routine. This was essential to fit in all I had set out to achieve. Compiling vision boards and really pushing myself out of my comfort zone was a major stepping stone also. Whether it was setting up my first cafe or doing a Tough Mudder race, Pat always helped me aim higher. The stronger my mind-set became, the less I feared failure. I now have very definite goals and a vision of where I want to go.

As my journey progressed, it included a lot more education, attending seminars and meditating. Another major shift came from taking time out – despite being busy – to just be really grateful and to reach out to help others in need.

Changing my mind-set has led to the biggest impact. I no longer live in suffering. I lean into all my pains and struggles now and I have tools set up to help me get back to where I need to be, as life is a journey and we never really know what's next. Nothing will hold me back now I believe as I have been released from my own self, which held me back – Pat released me for sure.

CHAPTER 3

SETTING THE GOAL

*'People usually overestimate what can be done in a day
and underestimate what can be done in a lifetime.'*
– Bill Gates, American business magnate,
entrepreneur and philanthropist

U ber investor Chris Sacca published a great story on the website
Medium about his friend and colleague, Uber CEO Travis Kalanick.
It's one that always springs to mind whenever I talk about setting goals
and the importance of focusing obsessively on smashing them. According to Sacca, when Uber was still in its infancy, Kalanick stayed with him
and his family over the holidays. One morning, as the family were hanging
out, Sacca's dad decided to break out the Nintendo Wii for a game of
virtual tennis and challenged Kalanick to join him. Kalanick, who, Sacca
recalls, was 'barely awake' at the time, agreed.

From the get-go, the Uber entrepreneur practically annihilated Sacca's
dad in spite of the fact that he didn't appear to be exerting much effort,
whereas Sacca's dad, on the other hand, was giving it his all. Kalanick was
winning every game. In fact, for the entire time they were playing, Sacca's
dad didn't score a single point, despite being a pretty skilful tennis player
and no stranger to Wii Tennis! He was flabbergasted by the defeat, and no
doubt silently questioning if his own skills were starting to dwindle.
At that point, Sacca recalls, Kalanick smiled and navigated the controller
over to the Wii settings page where there was a list of world rankings.
'I have a confession to make, Mr Sacca,' he began. 'I've played a fair

amount of Wii Tennis before. In fact, on the Wii Tennis global leaderboard, I am currently tied for 2nd in the world.'

Kalanick was literally the second best player in the world at Wii Tennis. It was at that point that Sacca realized Kalanick's intense obsession when it came to achieving a goal. Despite working around the clock on what is now one of the world's biggest transportation companies, he still focused obsessively on the Nintendo Wii Tennis because he had set a goal to be number 1 in the rankings.

This story came to light after Google announced they would be launching a rival to Uber. Upon learning of the news, Sacca tweeted that while he considered Google's Larry Page to be a genius, he would 'never, ever want to compete with Travis Kalanick'. Naturally, the tweet led to a barrage of questions from the media as to what Sacca had witnessed of Kalanick's personality that inspired him to fear competing with the Uber founder. Sacca explained that taking on Kalanick was a 'losing proposition', and shared the Wii Tennis story as testament to that. He wrote: 'If he [Kalanick] decides he wants to research a new industry, he will be a veritable expert within days. If he wants to understand a new city, he will be there 24 hours from now with just a half-sized backpack and already hanging with the locals. If he wants to be one of the best Wii Tennis players in the world, even while busy co-founding one of the fastest growing companies in history and advising a half dozen others from his storied Jampad, just give him a couple of weeks.'

Maybe this is an extreme example, but it's a necessary insight into the mind-set of a business (and a Wii Tennis!) sensation. It didn't matter to Kalanick if the goal was building an internationally successful company or reaching number 1 in a computer game ranking, the intensity of the focus remained the same once the goal was set. This is the focus you need to adopt if you want to radically change your life. Before we get to that, however, we need to complete the important process of setting the goal, which can be done following these five steps.

Step 1 the end vision

'The best decision you can make is the right decision, the second decision you can make is the wrong decision. The worst decision you can make is no decision. Take control of your own life.'

Pat Divilly

Most people never take the time to establish a clear vision of exactly what they want. They work and they work, but they don't know what they are working towards. If you fail to clarify EXACTLY what you want from your life, then you will just end up with the scraps of what everyone else didn't want. You are the most important person in the world, why would you settle for scraps? That's not a selfish way of thinking. If anything, it's vital you think this way because the reality is that no one else is going to look after you or come and save you.

Step one of achieving any goal is to get as specific as possible on what the goal is. You must also set the date you want to have it achieved by. When I decided I was going to raise €100K for Cystic Fibrosis Ireland, I immediately decided on a date it would be raised by: 5 October 2014. Not only did we reach the deadline we had set ourselves, we also ended up raising €165,000.

Most people are inclined to obsess over every little detail before committing to an end date, but this is also the reason why most goals are never seen through to fruition. You have to pick the vision, and not 'pick it apart', before you fully understand how you're going to get there. I had no idea how I was going to raise €100K. I just knew I was going to do it. Once I put it out there and made myself accountable, things started to happen for me. When you decide on something, everything else starts to align.

Here's how the art of goal setting works. If you decide roughly what you want, you might get somewhere close, but if you get real specific, then you have the best chance of getting there fast. The analogy I give to those who attend my seminars is that if they are travelling from the other side of the world to visit me, they will need a map. If they have a map of Ireland, they have some hope of finding me but probably wouldn't. If they have a map of Galway, then they have a better chance of finding me. If they have a map of the village where I live, then they're definitely going to find me. That's how goal setting operates. The more specific you are about what you want, the more likely you are to achieve it.

'You can't hit a target you don't see.'

Damon John, FUBU entrepreneur

I want you to envision yourself 12 months from now. Don't just think about the material possessions you have collected. Think about how you are feeling. Are you happy and full of energy? Has your health improved? Are you content? Are you proud of the progress you made during the previous 12 months? Are you excited about the goals and plans mapped out ahead of you? OR, are you still working the same job and dreading each day? Are you still feeling unfulfilled? Do you wake each morning feeling like you haven't enjoyed a decent sleep? Do you feel like you have coasted by throughout the past 12 months? Are you still feeling sick and tired of where you are in life?

Obviously no one wants the latter, but what are you doing to ensure that won't be your situation in 12 months' time? For this next exercise, I want you to pick a goal related to any one of the key areas in your life, such as health, relationships, family, career, finances, etc and set the date you want to have it completed by.

You are going to need more space to think creatively as you make your way further into this book, so if you haven't already done so by now, get yourself a separate notebook. Ideally you should have a notebook specifically for goal setting. When I visit successful friends and acquaintances of mine I always laugh when I see their impressive stationery collections and the pride they take in all their notebooks and journals. Keeping notebooks specifically for goals is a common trend among successful people and one you should adopt.

UPGRADE YOUR LIFE NOW!

How do I want to feel 12 months from now?

Grabbing the bull by the horns

'Never leave it until tomorrow. Grab the bull by the horns and start TODAY.'

Michelle Mone, Ultimo entrepreneur

For your next exercise, I want you to write down one thing you want to achieve and the exact date you want to achieve it by. People often refuse to do this. They list a range of excuses, each one disguised as a 'reason'. They make statements like, 'well I need to do more research before I can commit to a completion date', or 'I don't have the time right now with the kids/job/etc, but next year I definitely plan to start working towards my goal'.

Their reluctance to commit to a goal usually stems from either an underlying fear of failure, or a fear that their dream may not be everything they imagined. We have all heard the old adage, 'never meet your heroes as you will only be disappointed'. Some people, unbeknownst to themselves, apply the same logic to their goals. They're afraid the reality won't match the image they have created. For some people, the possibility of realizing a dream is a driving force, but for others it has the opposite effect. As a result, they subconsciously sabotage their progress. Rather than taking a risk and just going for it, they hold off, convincing themselves they will achieve their big goal in years to come.

Remember what I said before about living in fantasy land? You might be wondering how you could possibly be subconsciously sabotaging your progress. When a person builds a picture in their mind of what the finish line looks like, part of them also becomes quite fearful. They don't want their pride injured should they fail to achieve their goal, but above all, they don't want to set themselves up for disappointment. As I explained in the previous chapter, the brain immediately recognizes this fear and so does everything in its power to prevent the person from venturing near this perceived danger. This is why some people *always* find excuses not to commit to their goals. They create the chaos that prevents them from progressing. They block their own opportunities. If this is your situation, then you need to resolve to make a change right now, because the sad reality is that the opportunities you are barricading yourself from could potentially change your life for the better.

You have to realize that the only way to break the cycle of excuses is to take action. For this next exercise, I want you to abandon all goal-oriented fears right now and decide on just one thing you want to achieve. Remember, you have been gifted with the luxury of free thought so you might as well think big. You have nothing to lose by doing so.

Immediate imperfect action

If the vision is clear enough, you won't need to know the exact plan or worry about what the next step will be. In my experience, as soon as

UPGRADE YOUR LIFE NOW!

My goal:

End date:

someone makes a decision to do something, they have motivation to start looking for a reason to make it happen. They just need to trust that things will happen for them.

> 'Everything is energy and that's all there is to it. Match the frequency of the reality you want and you cannot help but get that reality. It can be no other way, this is not philosophy. This is physics.'
>
> *Darryl Anka, artist*

Every time an amazing new company like Uber, Hailo, or Facebook pops up, millions will say 'I thought of that first!'

Ideas are free. Action is key here, as is decision. You need to consciously form the habit of going in the opposite direction of procrastination. How do you do this? By making decisions and taking action.

If you were to take action on your ideas and turn them into a reality, imagine how different a person you would be in 12 months from now. I guarantee you would feel happier, more motivated, and definitely more content and fulfilled. Now imagine how different your life overall would be 12 months from now. You have one life to live, so stop postponing the important things. You weren't put here to work 9–5 in a job you hate, pay taxes, and die!

Some people will use an excuse like, 'I can't because . . . I don't have enough money, time, etc.' Start with what you have. Ed Sheeran is a guy whose story best exemplifies what I mean. Ed was an awkward teenager who wanted to be a singing sensation, so he used what he had and got started. He took his guitar and went street busking. There's a famous picture of him standing on a corner on Shop Street in my home city of Galway singing to the passers-by. Fast forward 10 years or so and rather than still busking on the streets of Galway, he's selling out Ireland's biggest stadium for multiple nights. Starting out, Ed would not have known every step that was going to get him to that level of success, but he knew what he wanted and didn't let the lack of a game plan paralyse him. He held on to the big vision and took consistent steps to get there.

Look around the room you're sitting in right this very moment. Everything in it started out as someone's idea. Even the book you're reading started out as a whimsical notion. It didn't just become a book. It started as a goal and progressed from there. Sometimes the most unlikely places become the water-well from which the best ideas spring. Take the footwear company FishFlops, for example. The idea for this brand came about after a young child drew fish on an outline of a sandal on a piece of paper. The company enjoys millions of dollars in sales and it all started from a child's drawing!

Everything around you started out as a thought process that was followed up with an action. Unfortunately, most people use their thought process in a negative as opposed to a productive way.

Dreams and ideas are all crucial, but in the end it's the decision-making and action-taking that will shape your life.

Look back on your life to date and think about certain decisions you made – or didn't make – that have affected your current circumstances. We have all made significant decisions that have impacted our lives in some way. Right now, you can make a decision that will impact your future. You can decide to change and in doing so your life will fire off in a completely different direction than it would have had you made the decision to stay the same.

Start being mindful of the fact that the more decisions you make, the more in control you are of your life.

Meeting Jack

Everyone has heard of author Jack Canfield and his *Chicken Soup for the Soul* books. His creation has become a phenomenal success with over half a billion people worldwide having bought a copy from the *Chicken Soup* series, and his name having graced the *New York Times* bestsellers list an enviable number of times.

In 2015, I attended a seminar he was holding in London and afterwards myself and a number of others had the opportunity to go to dinner with him. It was one thing to attend his seminar and hear him speak but to sit across the table from him and speak directly to the man himself? Amazing! He didn't disappoint either.

I remember one of the things he emphasized was the importance of asking for what you want. All too often, people assume a door is closed to them, when really all they have to do is ask for it to be opened. Ask for opportunities, ask for your big break . . . whatever it is you want, ask for it!

When Jack stressed this, I decided to heed his advice there and then. I had brought along my first two books with me that night so I asked him if I could give them to him and if he had any advice on how I could go about joining him on the *New York Times* bestsellers list! He gladly accepted my books and gave me some great insights into his own experience, most of which I have since employed in my own life and career. I hope you take a lot from this chapter, but if you only take one thing, let it be this: don't shy away from asking for what you want.

Once the vision has been written . . .

'Action is the true measure of intelligence.'

Napoleon Hill, author

Once your goal is on paper, you have to decide on the first action. What's the first thing you can do to put the goal in motion? Action changes everything because action is the opposite of procrastination. Most people are caught up in procrastination but the moment some form of action is adopted, you set the ball rolling.

When we set the €100K goal for charity, the first action we undertook was posting a video to Facebook announcing our intention. This also made us accountable. When we posted that video, we had no idea how we were going to achieve the goal. Honestly, we didn't have a clue! Once we put our intentions out there, however, things started to fall into place.

The same thing occurred when I committed to the goal of completing a triathlon. This goal came about as a result of several conversations with a lady called Karen who was working in my local barber shop. At the time, Karen was training for a triathlon and whenever I went in for a haircut, she and I would always end up chatting about her training regime. Her level of commitment was so inspiring, it was downright infectious, so much so that every time we spoke, I would find myself promising to sign up for a triathlon. It dawned on me one day that I had been saying it for six months. Right there and then I promised Karen that the next time she saw me, I would have completed a triathlon. I had two options. I could either find a new barber shop . . . or stick to my word and complete the triathlon. Frankly, it seemed easier to complete the triathlon!

As I was leaving the barber shop that day, I googled upcoming triathlons and signed up for a sprint triathlon that was set to take place a few weeks later. I had the advantage of being fit thanks to my job, but on the flip side I couldn't swim! Yep, I had really backed myself into a corner on that one. After signing up for the triathlon, I booked 10 swimming lessons and underwent the lot in the space of 10 days. I didn't wait until I had perfected things like my breast stroke, my dolphin kicks, or my bilateral breathing, I learned what I could and made the best of the skills I picked up. Don't wait for everything to be perfect before you start. Take action and then figure it out as you go. It's the one piece of advice that I have always lived by, so it probably comes as no surprise to learn that one of my favourite quotes is, 'If somebody offers you an amazing opportunity but you are not sure you can do it, say yes – then learn how to do it later.'

If anyone knows this to be true, it's the person who gave us that famous quote in the first place, Richard Branson. Prior to establishing himself as an entrepreneurial juggernaut, Branson had every obstacle thrown at him. Even when one of his early enterprises appeared to be on the verge of defeat, his positive spirit never waned, and neither did his determination. One of the things I admire most about him is his relentless pursuit of challenges and fulfilment. He never allowed his dyslexia or lack of education to determine whether or not he should embark upon a career in magazine publishing when he was just shy of 17. He didn't allow his age to stop him either! Most people might feel they can't relate to a billionaire, but when you read about the journey that shaped the man behind the brand, you'll probably find you can relate more to Branson than people you actually know. His journey is proof that anyone can change their life if they have a clear vision of what they want to achieve and the gusto to go after it.

I want you to start putting his famous quote into action. Sign up to the race before you're ready. Commit to a course. Just do something that backs you into a corner and forces you to make a change. Once you take action towards your goal – even a miniscule action – you automatically set in motion your plan. Things come together, excitement builds, and you start to gain momentum.

When you take a chance, yes you will sometimes stumble, but don't let the risk of looking silly stop you from pursuing a goal. How many people laughed at Elon Musk when he said he was co-creating a system that would enable people to make payments online? Bet they weren't laughing when he sold PayPal for a gargantuan sum of money. Despite his business pedigree, his ambition to build self-driving cars, not to mention a community on Mars, were two more goals that were met with much bemusement and criticism. Has it stopped him? No. Musk dreams up ideas that can literally change the world and he has taken huge risks to make them a reality. He doesn't linger on how the public might react. He just goes for it, and people respect him more because of it.

Step 2 the why

Once you have set the goal, the next step is to establish the reason why this goal is important to you. I call this process, 'peeling the onion', because it involves you uncovering the layers to find out the real reason behind a particular goal. In my experience, the bigger the goal, the bigger the vision, the stronger the why. Initially, my 'why' for wanting to be successful stemmed from the experience of being unable to buy Christmas gifts for my family. That's a strong motivator never to be in that position again.

Late Starter, Big Ambition

The marathon runner Gerry Duffy is a good friend of mine and the story of his 'why' is one I have shared many times at my seminars.

Here was a guy who was 4 stone overweight and didn't start running until he was 27 years of age, and yet he went on to complete 32 marathons on 32 consecutive days. That's no easy feat. In fact, one marathon is a huge achievement, so to complete 32 in such quick succession seemed impossible at first . . . until Gerry proved it was anything but.

His 'why moment' occurred after he had his picture taken with his golfing hero, Seve Ballesteros. Looking at that photo, Gerry realized he was overweight and out of shape, and actually ashamed to show the picture to anyone. There and then he decided to do something about it. He started off by running ten minutes each day. Gradually, as the days turned into weeks, his daily run became a habit. His pace quickened, and his strength built up. To ensure his motivation never waned, he carried with him the photo with Ballesteros.

His 'why' was his greatest motivator and eventually it led to him completing 32 marathons on 32 consecutive days, while at the same time raising a huge amount of money for charity.

The underlying 'why' behind your goal is hugely important because it's going to be your core motivation. To establish your 'why', you have to ask the question three times so that you peel back the layers and uncover the real motivation that's lying underneath.

Example 1: I want to make one million pounds this year.

Why do you want to make one million pounds? *I want to have financial security.*

Why does that matter? *Because I don't want to have to worry about bills or be unable to afford nice things.*

Why does that matter? *Because when I was growing up, my parents were always stressed about money and I don't want my kids to grow up in that kind of environment.*

Example 2: I want to lose weight for a wedding.

Why do you want to lose weight for a wedding? *Because I want to look good.*

Why does that matter? *Because I want to be confident.*

Why does that matter? *Because I don't like how I feel in myself especially ever since I was bullied at school as a teenager.*

They say your 'why' should make you cry. That's when you know you have uncovered the real motivation behind your goal. A young teenager I met during a trip to Nepal told me she wanted to build schools in areas that had been affected by the earthquake. As she was telling me about her dream, she started crying. Her 'why' had made her so passionate that she couldn't help but cry as she talked about it. That's true motivation right there. I was so impressed by her determination, not to mention convinced of her ability to make the goal happen, that I have personally committed to helping her.

Another example I often give involves a lady I worked with on one of my retreats. One day she shared with me her aspirations to obtain an MBA. When we peeled back the layers, we discovered her main motivation was to vex her father who always told her she wasn't good enough academically. Her breakthrough moment occurred when she realized that even if she went ahead and invested her time, energy, and money into obtaining this qualification, she still wouldn't feel fulfilled because an MBA wasn't something she genuinely wanted. It meant nothing to her. She was only embarking on the journey to try to prove someone else wrong. Your 'why' needs to mean something to you.

Initially my own 'why' stemmed from being unable to buy Christmas gifts for my family. In my seminars, I always like to share the example of a female client of mine who wanted to give up smoking but could never do it. As soon as she fell pregnant, however, she immediately quit smoking because her 'why' was now so strong. This was her leverage point. Now carry this across to your goal. What is your why? More importantly, is it strong enough?

Terry Fox's 'Why'

Canadian athlete and cancer research activist Terry Fox had one of the strongest 'whys' imaginable.

After suffering from knee pain for some time, he was diagnosed with a form of cancer called osteosarcoma in 1977. Unable to save the leg, doctors told him they would have to amputate and afterwards he would need to undergo months of chemotherapy. At the time, Fox had a 50% chance of survival. However, he learned that had his illness occurred two years earlier, that figure would have been less than 20%. This was his first stark realization of the importance of cancer research. Following the amputation surgery, Fox was fitted with an artificial leg. Armed with a phenomenally positive attitude towards his trying situation, he started to take back control of his life. As he progressed with the chemotherapy, he found it difficult to watch other patients succumb to the disease. His time in hospital made him realize just how little money was being invested in cancer research. Owing his own survival to the advances made in the research of the disease, he set about planning ways in which he could raise awareness as well as inspire others who were battling the illness, while at the same time raise some much needed funds. After some consideration, Fox decided he was going to put his artificial leg to good use and run the length of Canada.

His goal was enormous, but the 'why' behind it was gargantuan. Fox had witnessed fellow patients lose their lives to cancer and felt it was his responsibility as a survivor to raise awareness. His financial goal was $24 million, but rather than feel overwhelmed, he simply broke it down and said he wanted just $1 from each person in Canada, which at the time had a population of 24 million. In 1980, he set off across Canada in what was labelled the Marathon of Hope. As his one-man marathon progressed, so too did the publicity for his end goal and consequently many donations.

One hundred and forty-three days into his marathon, Fox was forced to bring his goal to a premature end as his cancer had spread to his lungs. Undeterred he planned to complete his goal once he had overcome the disease. Even when gravely ill, his 'why' kept him motivated. Sadly, by that time, the disease had spread too far into his body to be beaten and Fox fell into a coma nine months later before passing away. Since his passing, the annual Terry Fox Run has taken place in countries around the world, all in aid of cancer research, and as a result over $650 million has been raised. One man's remarkable 'why' literally motivated thousands of people and in turn made an enormous impact on something as important as cancer research.

Step 3 the brakes

Most people in business and life have their foot on the accelerator but their other foot is on the brake, and this is exactly what is holding them back. Once you take your foot off the brake, however, you can move towards your goal. The best way to do this is to identify the things that have stopped you from progressing in the past.

Whenever people set out to do something they previously failed at, such as giving up smoking or going to the gym, they have two choices. They can either ignore everything that went wrong before or look at what went wrong and figure out what their response will be if things start to go awry this time around.

If you are running a business but feel your lack of organizational skills may be holding you back, then don't assume that this will ever change. If you can identify it as a 'brake' and hire someone who is organized and can help you get things in order, then you are effectively taking your foot off the brake and accelerating forward.

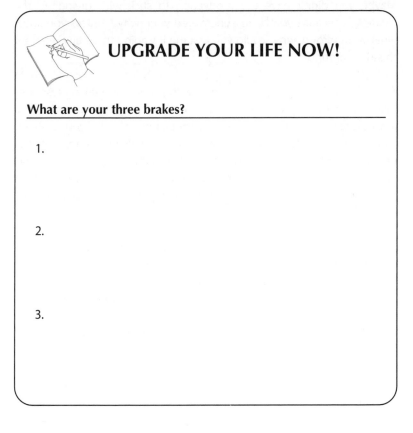

UPGRADE YOUR LIFE NOW!

What are your three brakes?

1.

2.

3.

For most people, 31 December is the day they make the same personal and professional New Year's resolutions. The zeal of the newly reformed kicks in and plans are plentiful, but come 31 January, those good intentions are long forgotten and instead old habits are reinstated. Remarkably, few people ever consider *why* their resolutions didn't work. They don't identify the brake. If you reflect on what went wrong the previous time you attempted to make a drastic change to your life, then you can adequately decide on how to prevent history from repeating itself.

Maybe when you last tried that diet, you didn't have time to meal prep? Maybe you didn't have the motivation to stick with giving up the cigarettes because you hadn't uncovered your 'why'? Unless you know what went wrong, why would you assume it's going to be any different this time around?

Again, it comes down to being honest with yourself and taking responsibility for why things went wrong before. One of my favourite pieces of advice is to prepare for the worst but to hope for the best. If you're late for a business meeting, you can promise yourself it will never happen again, or you can put a plan in place in case it does happen again. Most people react to things because they have no response. They will say they didn't see it coming. If you consider the fact that it *might* happen, however, then you can plan accordingly.

> 'It is not that we have so little time but that we lose so much. . . . The life we receive is not short but we make it so; we are not ill provided but use what we have wastefully.'
> *Lucius Annaeus Seneca, Roman Stoic philosopher*

For a lot of people, a major brake is their lack of time management.

Here's the secret to productive time management – it can only happen once you become completely aware of how you are spending and wasting it.

When my business was growing, I felt a little overwhelmed by the workload and consequently strapped for time. I was always busy and constantly working but yet I could never seem to get on top of the workload. When I reached out to a mentor for guidance, he had me complete a task. This was actually the first task he made me carry out. On an Excel spreadsheet I had to section the following 24 hours into slots of 30 minutes. The idea of this was that after every half hour, I would write in exactly what I did during that timeframe. I had been telling myself how busy I was but when I carried out this task, I realized that I was not as busy as I thought, I just wasn't utilizing my time effectively. This exercise makes you so much more aware of how you are spending your time. This is a particularly good exercise for a small business owner who might be struggling to get a handle on their day.

When I carried out the exercise, I realized I was spending around six hours a day on social media! Yes, social media is a huge part of my business but that exercise made me realize that I needed to be more efficient when on social media. It's so easy to get distracted by your newsfeed, but this distraction is where all those 'scrolling' minutes throughout the day turn into hours when combined! Realizing that I was spending six hours on social media made me ask myself if everything I did online during that timeframe was bringing in money, moving me forward in some way, or if it could be better spent?

I would recommend carrying out this exercise for two to three days if possible. Go about your day as normal so that you have a brutally honest reflection of where your time is being wasted. Don't change your routine just to make it look good on paper!

Once you have finished the exercise, you can look at the priority tasks that need to be carried out by you and the tasks that can be delegated or eliminated. Say, for instance, you spend five hours a week cleaning your house. This is a chore that can be delegated, so if you can afford it, consider the option of employing a cleaner. Straight away you have freed up five hours.

Once you have delegated certain tasks, eliminated the time wasters and freed up your time, I want you to keep on track by managing your time more carefully. To-do lists are all well and good but I want you instead to start making 'outcome lists'. What is the outcome you hope to have achieved by the end of the day or month? Don't get absorbed in your to-do list. Our to-do lists are often filled with menial tasks, but when you ask yourself what outcome you are trying to achieve, it brings you back to the core purpose of what you are doing, thus keeping you on track.

Of course, if a to-do list is how you like to keep on top of things, then by all means continue it, but I would recommend that you look at utilizing a very effective website such as www.todoist.com. This site allows you to make lists for each day as well as plan ahead. It will also remind you via email each morning what you have set out to do that day. As you complete each task, you simply tick it off the list. A great thing about this site is that it will even show you the stats on your productivity based on your site activity and how many tasks you tick off each day.

Step 4 your team and resources

Regardless of how big your vision may be, there's a 99% chance someone has already done it. The only exception I can think of is Elon Musk's aforementioned endeavour to build a community on Mars. Apart from that though, there's pretty much a template for everything!

Once you have identified your vision, you have to figure out who or what will help you fast track your way towards achieving that goal. Their journey becomes your template. Let's bring it down a notch and say your goal is something like learning a new language. You probably already know of someone who has done this, and you will definitely be able to find books authored by people who have mastered a new language in what seems to be an impossibly short length of time. All of these people are potential mentors. I'm sure there's no shortage of groups on Facebook either. Maybe you could join one and find a mentor there?

Tomatoes and Time Management

Set your tomato timer

When it comes to time management, I personally like the Pomodoro Technique, named after the tomato-shaped kitchen timer used by the creator Francesco Cirillo. This involves working for 25 minutes and then taking a break for 5 minutes. That counts as 1 Pomodoro. Maybe the break could involve grabbing a coffee, or checking texts and social media. Employing the Pomodoro Technique prevents the usual distractions from constantly creeping into your work time and hindering your productivity. You should also set objectives for each Pomodoro.

Here's an example of three Pomodoros I set:

Pomodoro 1
25 minutes – Read and edit a chapter from my book
5 minutes – Check my emails

Pomodoro 2
25 minutes – Schedule my Facebook updates for the week
5 minutes – Make coffee

Pomodoro 3
25 minutes – Make at least four sales calls
5 minutes – Check personal social media

When you divide your day like this, you can work so much more efficiently and your productivity will reach new heights. If you lack self-discipline or find yourself easily distracted, then a technique like this will make a considerable difference to how you spend your time.

When employing the Pomodoro Technique, you can write or type your objectives, but there are a number of Pomodoro sites online. Just Google the words 'Pomodoro Timer' and you'll see what I mean. One of the sites, www.tomato-timer.com, has a 25-minute stop clock that will notify you once the 25 minutes are up. Sites like these are free so use them!

Mentors and coaches are wonderful, but so too are books, audio books, DVDs, podcasts, online courses, and training programmes. If money is tight, check your local library for books that may be of benefit. There are all sorts of training materials and resources out there to help fast track the learning curve.

When I was starting out in the fitness industry, I was 22 years of age and fresh out of college. My vision was to be a personal trainer who could give clients all the information they needed. Unfortunately, my knowledge of nutrition was limited, and my finances even more so, which meant that undertaking additional courses was not an option at that point. However, I figured that if I read books by all the top personal trainers, then I would effectively 'download' some of that knowledge into my own brain and be able to use it in my career. It's about starting where you are, and working with what you've got, and that's exactly what I did, and still do. I really believe there are no excuses these days. After all, the internet alone enables you to link up with people from all over the world who have already done whatever it is you want to do.

'If you're prepared, and you know what it takes, it's not a risk. You just have to figure out how to get there. There is always a way to get there.'

Mark Cuban, billionaire businessman

You will often hear people in business talk about the importance of having mentors. I have had mentors in the past and found them to be an amazing source of advice and information. Even just taking someone to lunch and picking their brain for half an hour is a great way to fast track everything else.

When I set out to do my TEDx talk, I started thinking about who I could turn to for advice. Who had the template I could follow? I contacted both Gerry Duffy and Jack Kavanagh, two friends of mine who had graced the TEDx stage in the past. Both gave me valuable advice on how to structure my talk and in doing so completely changed my outlook and helped me feel far more prepared.

While mentors will tell you how they reached *their* goal, coaches on the other hand will guide you towards *your* goal and keep you on the right path until you get there. My friend Dax always likens mentors to bus drivers and coaches to taxi drivers. A bus driver, he says, is like a mentor. They decide the route you'll be travelling to get to your destination as they have already travelled that route themselves and know it's one that works. Taxi drivers, on the other hand, are like coaches. They will take you to where you want to go but you are the one calling the shots on how you want to get there.

'Think back 5 years ago. Think of where you're at today. Think ahead 5 years and what you want to accomplish. Be unstoppable.'

Dwayne 'The Rock' Johnson, actor, producer, and semi-retired professional wrestler

My goal at the moment is to become a strong swimmer, so I decided to employ the services of a swimming coach. She has helped me progress fast; much faster than I would have managed on my own. I train with a friend and we have become each other's accountability partners. If discipline is your weak point, then it really helps to have an accountability partner in whatever you do. This is a person that will help keep you motivated and refuse to listen to any excuses you come up with. The accountability partner I have for my swimming lessons keeps me right on track.

UPGRADE YOUR LIFE NOW!

List five people that can help accelerate your learning.

1.

2.

3.

4.

5.

Step 5 break down the goal

If your goal is a quite a big one, then it's crucial that you break it down as much as possible. This diminishes the daunting nature of the goal, thus suddenly making it more achievable. Trust me, even the biggest goal in the world becomes less overwhelming once broken down.

Maybe you want to make a million pounds in a year? Break it down into targets. To earn a million in a year, you would need to be earning £83,333 in a month, £19,230 in a week, or £2,739 in a day.

Want a top of the range sports car or a new house? Find out the price of the exact model you want. Let's say it's £200,000. To afford one in a year, you would need to be making £16,000 each month, £3,846 each week, or £548 each day.

Once you have broken it down, what next? Take it a step further, of course! Work out what you would need to do in order to earn the daily amount.

Let's take the goal of buying a £200K car/house. In order to make the daily goal of £548, you would need to be selling a product worth £25 to 22 people.

See what I mean when I say break it down as much as possible? Earning £16,000 in a month doesn't appear quite achievable. On the other hand, selling a £25 product to 22 people each day seems far more realistic.

Whether you have a shop, a website, or a seller's account on eBay or Depop, there's absolutely nothing stopping you from starting right now and making that dream happen. Another example of breaking down a goal comes from those who dare to battle the heights of Mount Everest. Climbing Everest is an enormous undertaking, both physically and mentally, but those who do it don't just set off aiming for the top. They aim for base camp, then their next goal is to reach camp 1, followed by camp 2 and camp 3. It's only when they have reached camp 4 that they then aim for the summit. The key to tackling any big goal is simple . . . just focus on the next target.

> 'I've learned that it doesn't matter how many times you have failed. You only have to be right once. I tried to sell powdered milk. I was an idiot lots of times, and I learned from them all.'
>
> *Mark Cuban, billionaire businessman*

Weight loss is a goal that people often find difficult to break down. I had a personal training client who wanted me to help her lose 10 stone over the coming year so she could look her absolute best in time for a family wedding.

This particular client had struggled with her weight all throughout her life, so in her eyes the 10-stone goal seemed like an intimidating target. On her very first day, we set manageable targets and in doing so changed her perspective on the journey she was about to undertake. We decided we would start by aiming for mini milestones, before progressing to slightly bigger milestones such as a two-stone loss, then four stone, and so on. She hit the goal through consistency, and because we had broken it down so much, at no point did she become overwhelmed.

A lot of people want to jump from A to Z. Rather than trying to go from couch potato to fitness model overnight, think of it as going from A to B, then C, and so on. Maybe each step could bring with it a new habit? In keeping with the subject of weight loss and fitness, some new habits could include drinking an extra litre of water a day, or hiking an extra mile. Adding productive new habits along the way will always help speed up the process.

I always say the journey towards a big goal is no different to that of climbing a mountain. It's tough and enduring but if you want to get to the top then you have to plan for a number of stops along the way where you can take a break and reflect on the progress you have made. Look at your goal and work out where along the journey the stop-off points should be. Set those targets but make them manageable.

Don't attach all your happiness to your goal

I'm going to end this chapter on what I believe to be a hugely important, but-all-too-often-forgotten, piece of advice: don't attach all your happiness to your goal. As an entrepreneur, I know what it's like to be so focused on a goal that it borders on obsession. With this level of focus often comes a lack of balance. It's so important to maintain a balance between having a big goal for the future, and being happy, content, and grateful in the present. When in the pursuit of big ambitions, it's all too easy to attach your happiness to whatever dream you're chasing. This is something we're all guilty of, but it's a habit that needs to be broken. Don't postpone your happiness to some far off point in the future and don't let your work dictate your mood. Your goal should be a compass that is guiding you towards personal growth, and not a barometer of happiness in the present. I have often seen this with weight loss clients. They sign up for a 90-day weight loss plan and expect to feel happier/ sexier/more confident on day 91 when the weight has been shed. Rather than wait until day 91, however, I always say you should try to figure out ways in which you can immediately start to feel happier/sexier/more confident. That way, you can start to enjoy the journey towards your goal.

The 26th Mile

In November 2015, I participated in a 24-hour adventure race in the Las Vegas desert alongside my friends Thomas Palmer and Kevin Clery. I wouldn't describe myself as a big fan of running. In fact, I wouldn't have even considered myself a runner but this was primarily because I had always *told* myself I wasn't a runner. The negative self-talk had me convinced that running was not for me. The reality was that I had never actually committed myself to becoming a runner.

As you can well imagine, the idea of a 24-hour race was a bit intimidating, especially to a self-diagnosed non-runner like myself, but we broke it down and focused on taking one hour at a time. We divided the day into manageable sections and figured out when we would stop to eat or to change into wetsuits. By incorporating these mini stops along the way, suddenly the race seemed a lot less daunting.

The adventure race was in aid of the suicide prevention charity Pieta House, and the motto of their campaign was the rather apt statement, 'Keep moving forward.'

That's exactly what Thomas, Kevin and I did for the entire race. We didn't focus on the finish line, we just concentrated on the next stop-off point. That's what we worked towards, and as a result that's what worked in our favour.

Adopting this mind-set also allowed us to enjoy the moment. We didn't postpone our happiness until we had finished the race, we embraced the moment – as gruelling as it was – and enjoyed it.

I always like the way Gerry Duffy explains it: 'Everyone wants to get to mile 26 in the marathon, but when you're on mile 9, just realize you need to get to mile 10 and then 11.'

⚠ Chapter 3 Cheat Sheet to Upgrade Your Life

- Once you have decided on a goal, you have to decide on the first action to put in motion the journey towards the goal.
- Action changes everything!
- If you are caught up in the destructive habit of procrastination – and most people are – the best way to fight it is to take some form of action. It doesn't matter how small the action may be, the cycle of procrastination is cut the moment action is adopted. Remember that.
- You will immediately remove the daunting nature of a big goal if you break it down into small targets. Break it down until it seems realistic to you.
- Don't attach all your happiness to your goal. By doing so, you are merely postponing your happiness. Instead, concentrate your happiness on the present moment.
- Once you have broken down your goal into manageable targets, forget about the finish line. Just concentrate on reaching the next target.
- There is always a way to fast track your journey to your goal. Make a conscious effort to establish how you can fast track yours.
- Mastering the art of time management takes practice. There are a number of exercises that will help you, but I personally like the Pomodoro Technique.

Upgrading My Life: Tommy Palmer (client)

When I first met Pat, I was a late comer to the fitness world. I attended his seminars, listened to his advice, and implemented his points on how to progress from thinking about a goal, to breaking it down into manageable steps, to taking consistent steps towards it each day. It's an ongoing process.

My primary goal when I first met Pat was to lose weight and get fit. At the time I was 49 and was about 3 stone overweight. I couldn't run 100 yards without being out of breath. Primarily my main concern was losing the weight and getting the fitness level back up. Thanks to Pat's advice, I more than exceeded my original goal. Not only did I lose the weight, I also ended up training to become a personal trainer! I just got so bitten by the fitness bug. I embraced the goal and it was all down to Pat's ethos of thinking big, setting goals, and adopting a step-by-step approach regardless of how big it may seem at the start. When I first went to Pat with my goal of losing weight, never in a million years did I think that 2 years later I would be helping others do the same. That idea wasn't even in my head, but Pat has a great way of instilling belief in people.

CHAPTER 4

THE FIVE PILLARS OF A HAPPY, FULFILLING LIFE

'As soon as something stops being fun, I think it's time to move on. Life is too short to be unhappy. Waking up stressed and miserable is not a good way to live.'
    – Richard Branson, entrepreneur, investor, and philanthropist

F or as long as I can remember, I have studied successful people. I have always been fascinated by why some people achieve all the things they want while others continue to struggle. My conclusion is that there's a recipe for everything in life. Whether it's losing weight or earning more money, there's always a recipe you can follow; a template that can be used to achieve the goal you want. The recipe for a happy, fulfilling life is exactly what we are going to outline in this chapter. You might be thinking, 'I will be happy once I'm successful! Pat, give me the recipe for success.'

It doesn't work in reverse, I'm afraid. It's pivotal that you pay attention to the five pillars first and foremost. If you don't, then you won't have the energy to give to your job, your relationships, and your family. When I interviewed serial entrepreneur Sean Whalen for my podcast series, he explained that he lives by the expression, 'the king eats first'. Whether it's the king or the queen, the premise behind his statement is that if you don't look after yourself, how can you expect to give your best to everyone else in your life? By looking after your own mental and physical health, everyone around you will benefit. It's not selfish to want to look after yourself. It's the opposite! If you are in the best state physically and mentally, then you are able to give more and be more to those whom you care about most.

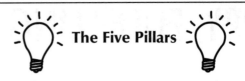

The Five Pillars

1. Health
2. Relationships
3. Career/Education/Finance
4. Adventure
5. Contribution

Once you have absorbed all the information in this chapter regarding the five pillars, the next chapter will outline how to implement the five pillars into your daily routine.

PILLAR 1: HEALTH

'You can't pay someone else to do your push-ups for you.' This quote by Jim Rohn is one of my all-time favourites. The logic is simple. If you want to enjoy good health, then you have to do the work yourself.

When I was training people on the beach, they were getting stronger physically but there were many other notable changes taking place as a direct result of that. They had gained a newfound confidence from fitness, which led to amazing transformations within both their personal and professional lives.

For me when it comes to health – the physical side of it anyway – it's about taking on new challenges. When I was growing up, my main focus was lifting weights and Mixed Martial Arts (MMA). At the time I was pretty passionate about MMA in particular. For a while I even wanted to be a cage fighter, but much to my mother's great relief that's no longer an ambition of mine! My new challenge is to learn how to swim properly. The more I progress with it, the more I can feel my confidence growing. It's easy to stick to what you know, which is fine if you enjoy it but are you stuck in the comfort zone? Could you be pushing yourself that bit more? For me, the comfort zone is lifting weights because I know what I'm doing. Swimming, however, is completely new and so I'm forced to push myself that bit more.

Here is what I recommend:

A: Physical activity

For three days each week, you should aim to carry out 30–45 minutes of vigorous exercise. The other four days should consist of 30–45 minute sessions involving rejuvenating exercises. Try if you can to complete the sessions in the morning so that they're not looming over you. Everyone is different; maybe you're a night owl and prefer the evening workouts. Go with whatever suits you best, but make sure to find something you enjoy. If you can, try to incorporate sporting activities that have a social element.

A lack of self-discipline can be the reason most fitness routines fall by the wayside in favour of an extra hour at the office or in front of the TV. This is less likely to happen if you get a coach. I know I probably wouldn't be half as consistent with my trips to the swimming pool if it were not for my swimming coach keeping me accountable. In fact, I probably wouldn't turn up at all. If you can't afford a coach or a personal trainer, sign up to a class. There is always a solution, so don't even try to entertain the excuses.

I would strongly recommend exercising your hardest in the morning. Remember, there's great value in suffering! Sounds strange but it's true.

If you go through a tough workout, the rest of the day is easy. That little bit of suffering you endured during the workout translates so far across the board. The trivial things that annoy others won't knock a flinch out of you.

It brings to mind Jim Rohn's quote again, 'You can't pay someone else to do your push-ups for you.' That's the great thing about fitness, it doesn't matter if you're the richest or the poorest, you have to do the work yourself if you want to enjoy the results.

I grew my fitness business from the ground up, and during that time I witnessed countless people change their lives through fitness. The challenges they embraced in the gym made them stronger physically and mentally. These people weren't bodybuilders or strict fitness fanatics. They were ordinary people who wanted to embark upon a regular fitness routine so they could get into the best shape possible and feel good about themselves. Fitness is not just about obtaining abs or muscle definition – it's about improving your energy levels so you can be your most productive self each day; it's about the feel-good factor you experience after completing a tough session. Don't use lack of time as an excuse. The busier you are, the more of a necessity a good fitness routine becomes. Fitness also plays a huge part in stress management, as does my next recommendation.

B: Meditation

'If a car is speeding at 100 miles an hour without braking, it's going to eventually crash or burn out. It's the same with the human body and mind. If you don't learn to slow down, you will crash and burn.'

Pat Divilly

Meditation is something that all high achievers practice in some form. I used to think it was for gurus, an up-in-the-air kind of practice, but once I experienced the benefits for myself, my whole outlook changed.

Meditation helps you become psychologically more bullet-proof. It helps you get to know yourself so you're not as fazed by external stimuli. People who are not comfortable in themselves are thrown by anything that is said to them.

Meditation helps us utilize the right part of the brain, which stimulates creativity, ideas, and solutions. Some of the greatest names in history devised their best ideas while sitting in a peaceful silence.

Many people reject the idea of meditation after the first attempt because they struggle to wipe their mind of any thoughts. This is not what meditation is about. It's about quietening the inner chatter that takes place all day. I remember reading a great tip about how to prevent the mind from wandering during meditation. I can't think of the man's name, but whenever he felt the inner chatter starting up, he would silently count the beads on his mala bracelet (mala beads are traditionally used the world over in prayer and meditation). This immediately brought his focus back to the present moment, allowing him to just 'be'.

When you meditate, leave your phone in another room. Resist the temptation to put it on silent and leave it nearby. You know only too well that you will jump up to check it as soon as you see the notification light flashing, or hear the vibration alert when a social media message comes through.

Meditation creates a barrier between you and stress, but this is just one of the many by-products of the practice. We are so responsive to the anxieties around us, but through meditation, the outside world becomes less noisy. Meditation introduces a sense of calm to life. When you practise meditation, you will notice a reduction in the level of chaos around you.

Through meditation, you become comfortable sitting in silence by yourself; you try new challenges without difficulty; you start to generate new ideas with ease; you find you are more focused at work and not as troubled by problems or obstacles . . . all of this and more stems from introducing some peace to a busy mind.

People are often intimidated by the idea of meditation because they think they have to be a yogi or a Buddhist, but that's not the case at all. A simple 10 minutes of meditation each day is going to help you better control your day and all the stresses that come with it. It's a small change that can make the biggest difference.

To get you started, I have uploaded a simple guided meditation to www.upgradeyourlifebook.com free for you to use. Just listen to it for 10 minutes each day and it will introduce you to greater levels of productivity and stress management. If you find yourself extra-stressed, then meditate for 30 minutes.

When you're feeling stressed or under pressure, try this breathing technique. Inhale for five seconds and hold for two before exhaling for a further eight seconds. You should feel a difference almost immediately but continue doing it until you notice a change in your stress and anxiety levels.

C: Nutrition

I'm not going to preach about nutrition here. Some people are vegan, some are paleo, some are vegetarian, and so on. Of all the nutritional plans that are out there, however, there's none that will argue against the merits of natural foods and vegetables. We need to recognize the direct link between the foods we eat and the way we think and feel. An unhealthy body simply cannot fuel a healthy productive mind, so, if you're feeling fatigued, anxious, irritable, and run down almost all of the time, then I can guarantee your daily diet is a huge factor in this. Changing the type of food you eat will make an enormous difference, and I have witnessed this first hand with the clients I have trained over the years.

I like the 80/20 rule. Stay strict enough 80% of the time but allow yourself to deviate 20% of the time. For prolonged energy, try to incorporate more healthy fats into your diet, things such as nuts, seeds, avocado, oils, and oily fish. Above all, cut back on the sugar. Sugar is a massive issue and as far as I'm concerned the enemy to good health and productivity in business. It will not give you the focus and energy you need to work effectively. Trust me, healthy fats are much better. If your sugar-rush of choice is a soft drink, I would strongly advise you to replace it with water. It goes without saying that hydration is vital for maximum productivity and clarity. Very often we reach for the coffee or the Coca Cola to help fight fatigue when in fact water is the fuel we're lacking, not caffeine.

When you wake up in the morning, you are at your most dehydrated, which is why you should keep a bottle by your bedside to drink from as soon as you wake. One particular client I coached used to complain of having no energy and great difficulty in focusing. I advised him to increase his intake of water and encouraged him to leave a bottle of water in his car, beside his bed, and in his office. I wanted him to develop the habit of drinking water more regularly, so I also advised him to replace all soft drinks with water and to take note of any changes in how he was feeling after a week or so. He was shocked by the difference it made.

Dehydration affects mental and physical performance, which is why it is so important to rehydrate often. You should also try to gradually increase your water intake from week to week. Add an extra glass here and there until you are drinking at least six to eight glasses per day. If you don't like plain water, experiment with natural flavours such as herbs, cucumber, or freshly squeezed lemon and lime, etc. And no, shop-bought flavoured waters are not advised! They are filled with sugar and offer no more health benefits than your average soft drink.

 Here are some healthy juices and smoothies I would recommend:

Silverstrand Sunset Juice
1 chopped carrot
1 diced mango (if you want an ice-cold smoothie, then freeze the diced mango for a few hours before making the smoothie)
1 pint of water. If using a Nutribullet, fill to the max line.
Now all you have to do is blend the lot until smooth.

Claddagh Concentration Boost
120g of frozen or fresh blueberries
225ml of almond milk
½ ripe avocado, skinned and pitted
1tbsp chia seeds
1tsp maple syrup
¼ tsp of cinnamon
Handful of ice
Now blend, blend, blend!

Barna Brain Fuel
1 large peach diced (don't forget to remove the stone!)
50g of kale washed and torn
1 tsp of unpasteurized apple cider vinegar

250ml cold coconut milk
Add to a blender and blitz!

Pat's Pina Colada Smoothie
1 cup of frozen pineapple chunks
2 tbsp of desiccated coconut
1 cup of coconut milk
1 scoop of banana protein powder
1 cup of ice
    Blend until the ingredients have fully mixed and the texture is smooth.

D: Sleep

A restful night's sleep is paramount for optimum productivity. Often, the media lauds business figures who claim to require very little shut-eye, but this is not something to aspire to. If you are serious about success, then sleep should not be something you postpone, it should be something you make a priority. Unfortunately, a restful night's sleep is something most of us crave but so few of us enjoy. It can be difficult to switch off. Sometimes, it can be downright impossible.

There are a number of solutions you can put to use, however.

Dr Andrew Weil, a Harvard-trained medical doctor who also specializes in holistic health, developed a brilliant technique for relaxing the mind and inducing a state peaceful enough to encourage sleep. It's called the 4-7-8 Technique and it has actually been touted as a technique that will help you get to sleep in 60 seconds, although it has never worked that fast for me. This is actually a great technique to employ whenever you're highly anxious and need to calm your nerves. I have used it myself many times.

When I first started out in public speaking, the nerves were tough to deal with so I looked into a variety of calming techniques and strategies. I eventually took control of my pre-talk nerves and anxiety by employing the 4-7-8 Technique. Before I go on stage, I close my eyes and carry out the technique five times or so. Almost instantly I will feel considerably calmer and more at ease. I should point out here that as well as carrying out the breathing technique, I also pay close attention to my internal dialogue and become mindful of the language I use. During the early days of my public speaking engagements, I used to dread going on stage. I would tell myself over and over that I hated it. As soon as I became more aware of how the brain processes such dialogue, however, I immediately changed the tone of my inner voice and started telling myself that I enjoyed public speaking. Combined with the breathing technique, the impact was significant and my nerves have since disappeared.

Whether you want to enjoy a good night's sleep or ease the anxiety before an important meeting, the 4-7-8 Technique is well worth a try.

Here's how you do it:

1. Place the tip of your tongue against the roof of your mouth, directly behind your upper front teeth and keep it there throughout the entire exercise.
2. Exhale through your mouth, making a 'whoosh' noise.
3. Close your mouth and inhale silently through your nose for 4 seconds.
4. Now hold that breath for 7 seconds.
5. Exhale through your mouth, while making the 'whoosh' noise, for 8 seconds.
6. This constitutes one breath. Repeat three more times so you have completed a total of four breaths.

According to Dr Weil, the most important part of the technique is holding your breath for 7 seconds. By holding your breath for this length of time, you are allowing your lungs to fill up with oxygen and circulate around the body thus producing a calming effect.

I would also recommend listening to good quality hypnosis tracks.

 At www.upgradeyourlifebook.com you will find a really beneficial guided meditation that my own clients love. They listened to it through headphones while lying in bed at night and it had a drastic impact on the quality of sleep they enjoyed.

There are many other ways in which you can encourage a restful night's sleep, but one of the most beneficial tips by far would be to switch off the phone. This is a tough one. Even I find it difficult! The blue screen on your phone simulates daylight, which in turn disrupts your natural circadian rhythm. The single best thing you can do to improve the quality of your sleep is to stop looking at your phone at least an hour before you go to bed. Your body cannot wind down naturally if the blue screen is stimulating your brain. The same goes for having a television on in your bedroom. If you nod off with a screen flickering in front of you, your quality of sleep will be poor at best.

There are also quite a lot of sleep sprays on the market that are designed to relax. It's tempting to overlook these as being gimmicky products but some people do find them extremely beneficial. I have heard great things about the sleep sprays from the brands 'It Works' and 'The Body Shop'.

PILLAR 2: RELATIONSHIPS AND NETWORKING

ABC: Always be connected

Regardless of how healthy you become or how high up the Forbes rich list you climb, the quality of your life is going to be largely defined by the quality of your personal relationships. Like anything else in life, relationships require work. Sometimes we take them for granted, and fail to see them becoming weakened over time.

This is why it is pivotal that you regularly develop and nurture existing relationships. Whether you are starting a new business or trying to climb the ladder in your current job, you shouldn't be sacrificing these relationships or taking them for granted.

There was a private coaching client of mine who was on the verge of divorce. When he told me about his circumstances, I told him to implement one simple change. I advised him to acknowledge his wife every day for 90 days. He came back to me afterwards and said she had completely changed when in fact it was he who had changed the way they interacted.

It's easy to fall too far into 24/7 work mode. I myself used to be guilty of this. The people that mattered the most, I took for granted. My business was built on relationships and treating people well, trying to be the best part of people's day, helping them go the extra mile. As a result of my commitment to my business, my personal relationships suffered.

They didn't have to, but I let them.

With personal relationships, you have to work on what you've got, and not take them for granted. Each morning, Vaynermedia CEO Gary Vaynerchuk phones his closest family members while in the car on the way to the office. I've met Gary – in fact I shared a stage with him – he's a supremely busy guy, but he makes a conscious effort to find the ideal pocket of time in his day to check in with those that matter most to him.

Meeting Dan

Dan Meredith was a guy I connected with some time ago on social media. I had been following his page Coffee with Dan and over a period of time we became friends. I was always fascinated by how he managed to build up such an amazing network of global entrepreneurs, and I couldn't understand how he did it until I met him in person for the first time this year. We walked around his small town and there wasn't one person he didn't speak with. He complimented people, he took an interest in those around him, and from the brief time I spent observing him, it quickly became evident that his secret lay in how he treated people. If you are not a natural conversationalist, you can train yourself to become one.

UPGRADE YOUR LIFE NOW!

Identify the relationships that require immediate attention and improvement.

Personal:

1.

2.

3.

Now I want you to think about one thing you can do, preferably on a daily basis, that will help improve these relationships.

Personal:

Person 1.

Person 2.

Person 3.

It doesn't have to be a grand gesture. It can be something as simple as arranging a weekly date night with your wife, or organizing a Skype call with a loved one who lives in another country.

Start making small talk with a shop assistant or conversing with the person standing next to you in a queue. If you go to the same coffee shop every day, try to slowly build a rapport with the barista. It will be difficult at first, especially if you are an introvert by nature, but it's all about breaking the habit. Don't think to yourself that you could never be as good a conversationalist as Dan. He's an amazing networker but he wasn't born that way, it was a trait he honed over time. I would consider myself to be somewhat of an introvert, so when I find myself baulking at the idea of randomly conversing with someone, I simply remind myself that it's just a smile and a few words. The world is a mirror and I always find that when you start smiling and talking to people, you get the same thing back in return. Don't wait for the other person to say hello or to smile, be the person who does it first.

To get you started, I want you to complete the following exercise but most importantly of all, I want you to see it through! I have also included five conversation starters that you can use.

 UPGRADE YOUR LIFE NOW!

List three people you see on a regular basis that you could start conversing with.

1.

2.

3.

Professional relationships: mastermind groups

When it comes to professional relationships, I want you to ask yourself, are you waiting or creating? If you're not actively going out and connecting with other people, how can you expect to grow as a business person?

Personally, I choose to be part of mastermind groups.

There are so many mastermind groups out there that would be of huge benefit to someone with a great drive to succeed. Being around like-minded people – the 'think big' brigade, if you will – really fires up the motivation to succeed.

The idea behind a mastermind group is to bring together like-minded people from different industries. Each member discusses their week's victories and losses and opens up about any struggles they have been experiencing. Each member has an 'ask' for the week. This could be something they are struggling with and need help with. This is where the power of the mastermind group will shine. If the group members are from a diverse range of professions, then chances are there will be a person in that group that will be able to help solve the problem in some way. They may be able to provide solutions from their own experiences in business or they may have a contact who can help. I often find it enormously helpful when the other group members offer their perspective on a situation.

Before the group breaks, each member commits to an action that they are going to have completed by the next mastermind meeting. This introduces an element of accountability into the equation. Once you have voiced your commitment, you have to see it through.

There are plenty of mastermind groups out there. Some groups are free to join, but in my experience the top quality groups come with a membership fee. The top quality groups are genuinely worth every cent. If people are paying to be in a mastermind group, they are serious go-getters who know what they want and are not interested in time-wasting. The more exclusive the group, the more expensive the fee, but the upside of this is that you get to enjoy more access to some incredibly influential people who can help you in a variety of different ways.

If you can't find a mastermind group in your nearest town or city, then take the leap and set up your own.

How to run your own mastermind group

- Decide how often your group will meet. Ideally you should be aiming to get together at least once or twice a month. Some groups meet once a week.
- Appoint a chairperson.
- Be strict with the group. Don't allow time-wasters to hijack proceedings.
- The chairperson should always start the meetings on a positive note by asking each member of the group what their victories were for the week. These can be personal or professional victories.
- Next, each member can share their struggles or problems they may be encountering. Ensure that each member has time to speak without being interrupted. Once they have finished speaking, allow the other members to put forward their own suggestions or solutions.
- The next stage of the meeting is 'the ask' where each member voices what they need help with that week.
- A mastermind meeting should always end on an action of accountability. Before the group breaks, each member should state one thing they are going to complete before the next meeting is held.

To find out more about my own private mastermind group, just head on over to www.upgradeyourlifebook. com.

Confrontation – turning a negative situation into a positive one

Your success in business and in life will essentially be determined by how well you deal with people. Even though meditation will help you deal with confrontational individuals, it's still tough if it's happening on a frequent basis.

One of my private coaching clients – let's call him Gary – worked in the kind of pressurized environment that was occupied by a lot of highly strung individuals. Heated exchanges and disagreements were an inevitable occurrence, but Gary wasn't a dog-eat-dog kind of guy and so had no idea how to handle these situations whenever they arose. As a result, his anxiety levels were through-the-roof and he started to dread a job he once loved.

Arguments do tend to introduce a negative energy that can affect you in more ways than you realize, and while you can't control the actions of another person, you can most definitely control how you respond to them.

Here are six tips on how to effectively handle this kind of negative situation:

1. When someone is venting, whether they be family, friend, work colleague, or staff, don't interrupt. Let them get it out of their system.
2. Once they have finished, take a pause and ask them if there is anything else they would like to add on. They will more than likely

reinforce a point they have already made, but at least now you know what they feel most upset about.

3. Arguments really flare up when both sides concentrate on a point of disagreement. If possible, try to place the focus on points of agreement.

4. Don't jump to conclusions. If there is a point they made that you wholeheartedly disagree with, ask them to clarify what they mean and then acknowledge it.

Don't take the confrontation personally. When you are trying to understand why a person is adopting a particular stance (or why they are taking umbrage in the first place), examine certain factors. What age group do they fall into? Maybe their age, aka generational view, is largely influencing their opinion? Maybe their personal life is in turmoil and they are taking their anger out on you? Maybe they don't feel as though they are being shown enough respect from others and confrontation is their way of standing their ground? There are many 'maybes' to be considered, but if you refuse to take it personally then you immediately eliminate any potential for it to poison your peace of mind. Everyone has their own personal turmoils that you know nothing about, so if someone in your workplace reacts in a negative way when dealing with you, remember it is not a reflection of you but rather a reflection of their state of mind.

5. Most heated arguments could be avoided if people simply made the effort to contain the volume of their voice. The louder the other person gets, the calmer your voice should become. It's hard for someone to continue shouting without feeling foolish when the other person involved is remaining calm, dignified, and composed.

6. Be mindful of the type of language you use. You may think you are coming across as considerate but the other person may interpret what you're saying as being patronizing. Rather than saying 'You're talking rubbish', say 'Help me understand where you're coming from on this topic.'

Instead of exclaiming 'No, you're wrong', try 'Can I outline my point of view on this?'

Dealing with your critics

If someone verbally attacks you in some way, whether it be your choices in life, your viewpoint on a particular subject, your relationships, or your career/business – and let's face it this is a pretty frequent occurrence on social media – obviously your natural reaction is going to be one of defence. Don't get defensive. Openly try to understand the situation from their viewpoint. People are less inclined to be as argumentative when the other party actively tries to understand their point of view. It's also pretty difficult for someone to continue shouting off in the face of manners and calm.

Of course, there's a fine line between someone who is voicing a legitimate complaint and someone who is blatantly abusing you. This is where meditation really demonstrates its worth. If you meditate frequently, you won't be fazed by the keyboard warriors. When I was running Pat Divilly Fitness, on occasion I would find myself on the receiving end of a diatribe of abuse from certain people. During the earlier days, I would try to defend myself and reason with the critics but I quickly realized that doing so only stimulated their venom even more. The whole exchange might last no more than a few minutes but it would leave me incredibly stressed. Even though I had hundreds of people praising my work, the negative remarks were the ones that plagued me. Meditation, however, released me from their grip. A negative comment no longer lingers in my mind or has the power to affect how I'm feeling. As I said in Chapter 2, the more you meditate, the more bullet-proof you become.

I'm also lucky in that I have a great personal network of people around me. If my family and closest friends appreciate and respect what I'm doing, then I know I'm on the right track. If, however, they say I'm doing something wrong, then I know I need to rethink things. Those are the people I trust and listen to, not the armchair critics. In business, it is always good to have a circle of people who can act as your soundboard and whose opinion you value.

These days most people find themselves competing with a phone for the attention of their loved ones. One of the greatest displays of respect you can show to another person is to just look them in the eye and listen. Don't side-eye your phone, the clock, or the television, just listen intently to the person speaking. When I spoke with Gary Vaynerchuk, I was so incredibly impressed by his character and the genuine interest he expressed in meeting with people. He may be the king of social media but when he's in company, he's very much engaged in conversing with those around him. I also noticed his tendency to treat the person in front of him as the most important person in the room. Gary always gives people his full attention. Do this for everyone you meet, and you will make one hell of an impression too.

'I've learned that people will forget what you said, people will forget what you did, but people will never forget how you made them feel.'

Maya Angelou, American poet, author,
and civil rights activist

The wow factor

If you currently run your own business, or if your goal is to be an entrepreneur, then this next section is 100% for you. Even though I address the topic from a business perspective, it goes without saying that the lessons throughout can also be applied to personal development. The wow factor can easily be implemented in areas such as relationships, home life, health, fitness, etc.

When I was running my fitness business, I was always big on having a wow factor. My ethos was always based on the fact that no commercial gym would do the things I was willing to do. In the early days I used to text clients to check that they had enjoyed the session. Of course, that wasn't practical for the future when my classes started growing in size. Instead I would utilize different forms of social media to stay in contact with my clients and provide them with whatever support they needed.

'All successful people focus on adding value to the service or product they provide. Add the value and the money will follow. Trust me on that one. It doesn't work any other way.'

Pat Divilly

Gill Carroll, the owner of my two favourite restaurants in Galway, 56 Central and 37 West, is a great advocate of implementing the wow factor and does so by allocating a daily allowance of €5 for each of her staff members. Each waiter and waitress can then use this individual allowance to treat a customer and make their day a little brighter. A staff member might choose to give someone a free cup of coffee or a brownie, but once they have done it, they have to write it on a blackboard in the kitchen. It's a very effective approach to adopt because it helps establish a culture of wowing the customer.

What I want you to do is put yourself in your client's shoes and ask yourself how you can wow them. Maybe you can take a day in the month where you send out a thank you card or a small gift as a gesture of good will. Little things that make you stand out. Take 20 minutes right now to brainstorm how you can add more value to your business.

When I started out training the initial five clients, I figured they were probably not being acknowledged that much in their work or home life. People forget to encourage and acknowledge each other, but I live by the philosophy that a little word of encouragement can make a big difference. The class grew to over 100 people in three months and 500 people thereafter. To me, it wasn't the exercises that were attracting the clients, but rather the interactions and the way I treated people. In a world where everyone is obsessed with Facebook marketing and Twitter marketing, we have lost touch with personal interaction.

When I was 18 years of age and fresh out of school, I travelled to America with aspirations to become a cage fighter. Mixed Martial Arts was a passion of mine as a teenager, so once those school doors shut behind me, I headed off to San Diego on my own and joined a gym called Undisputed, which was run by Ryan Johnson. Ryan took me under his wing and it was in his gym that I witnessed an incredible culture of teamwork where the people you trained alongside became your best friends. There were always nights out, social get-togethers to watch boxing fights, we'd go for food together, all sorts of things like that. I didn't realize it at the time, but we were just like a family. That's the kind of environment that was developed and nurtured in Undisputed. When I started my classes on the beach six years later, I strived to recreate that same culture. Each Friday after our class, my clients and I would go for a coffee together. Once a month, we would enjoy a night out to celebrate the results the clients had achieved. Those were just two of a number of things we would do together, and the impact was incredible. A real sense of community developed and it became more than just a training group.

Ask yourself how you can introduce this same sense of culture to your employees and customers? How can you make them all feel as though they are part of a community? Let's look at a big corporation such as Facebook. When I visited San Francisco in October 2015, I was brought out to the Facebook headquarters and given a personal tour of the place. The interior of the HQ itself was phenomenal but even more amazing was witnessing how the staff interacted with each other and how Facebook had managed to introduce such a culture of comfort on such a huge scale. You could tell that the employees all felt 'at home'. They felt supported and appreciated. The on-site facilities supported their work/life balance, which meant employees were happy and content as opposed to stressed and miserable. Facebook and Google are two companies famous for their employee-focused culture.

Yes, these corporations have big budgets in place to make life comfort-able for their employees but that doesn't mean you cannot take inspiration from how they operate. The wow factor implemented by Gill in her restaurants is a prime example of how you can create a distinctly positive culture on a smaller scale.

At no point should the core message here be forgotten. It's not about giving away free stuff or making life super-comfortable for your staff. It's about how you make people feel. How can you make your staff feel good about themselves? How can you make a customer's day a bit brighter so that they leave feeling happy?

I recently returned to Mixed Martial Arts. Not that I have ambitions of stepping into the ring or anything like that, but as MMA was such a passion of mine as a kid, I decided to pick it up again. I visited a couple of gyms hoping to experience the same culture I had witnessed in Ryan Johnson's gym some years back, but no such luck unfortunately. There was no sense of culture in any of the gyms I visited and as a result I just couldn't get back into the swing of things. I can totally understand why people so easily lose the motivation to continue going to the gym. When there's no culture, there's nothing to keep you there. It may seem like an unlikely source of inspiration, but those cage fighting days in San Diego taught me a lot about the importance of creating a culture where people felt welcome.

The company with the best culture is not the one that hands out company cars like free lunches, nor is it the one with the expensive office furniture and interior design. It's the one where the staff enjoy working together and each of them feels as though they are a valued member of the company.

One of the ways in which you could do this is to integrate a culture of personal development where every so often you buy your employees books that will help motivate and empower them. Maybe they could have an education budget where they can buy the books they would like to read? Or perhaps a few of their working hours could be allocated to education?

Chat to your staff and find out what's on their bucket list. When the time comes to reward them for a job well done, you could give them bucket list experiences. It's about developing a culture where employees feel appreciated.

It's important to instill the same culture amongst your client base. There is a company in the States called Zappos. They have created such a phenomenal culture amongst customers and potential customers that the company is renowned for having one of the best customer care teams in the world. If a person contacts them looking for a product they don't have, they will search Google for a stockist of the product in question. They will then ring the person back and give them information about the stockist, even if it's one of their competitors. That's how far they go with their customer service. Zappos staff go to these lengths for the customers because that's the culture created within the company. However, a positive change absolutely has to start at the top before it can work its way down to the staff and then the customer. Unhappy customers are usually a good indication of unhappy staff, so it's important that you look at how you can support your employees and ensure they are content in their place of work.

When a new employee arrives at the office on their first day, make a point of celebrating their first day. Give them a list of the best places to have lunch, get coffee, etc. Make them feel part of the workplace community. If you can, get them a welcome gift, maybe a lunch voucher. That's how you welcome people to your company. Straight away they are off to a positive start and feel appreciated and valued. Give the new employee a reason to tell people how amazing it is to work for your company.

Is it necessary for your employees to work 9–5? If an employee is turning up stressed and depressed because of the traffic-heavy commute into work, then maybe they could work from home for the first hour or so? I would rather have an employee turn up at 11am happy, content, and prepared for a productive day ahead than to have them turn up at 9 on the dot, stressed, miserable, and wishing they were anywhere else but at their desk. You won't get the best from an employee if they're in that state of mind.

Whether your team consists of two people or 200, I would strongly recommend that you develop a good knowledge of each individual.

What are the fears and anxieties of your employees? Do you know what they are worried about? Do you know what they love? Or even what motivates them? When you get to know your employees on that level, your company will grow beyond what you ever envisioned. This is what comes from caring for the person behind the employee.

Look at the strengths of your employees, look at where in the business they thrive best. What are their dreams and ambitions? What's on their bucket list? Do you know their goals? And more importantly, do *they* know your vision?

Sometimes we as business owners almost expect those around us to read our minds. We expect our team to understand our ideas. If you have never fully communicated your vision to your staff, how are they going to know exactly what they should be working towards? Entrepreneurs sometimes find it difficult to communicate their vision to their staff but it's important that you do so.

Don't bark orders at your staff, show them your vision and inspire them to follow. There's a quote by the novelist Antoine de Saint-Exupery that really encapsulates how it should be done. He explains that the best way to build a boat is not to have your staff collect bits of wood but rather show them the vastness of the sea you want to sail.

'If you want to build a ship, don't drum up people to collect wood and don't assign them tasks and work, but rather teach them to long for the endless immensity of the sea!'

Antoine de Saint-Exupery, writer and poet

Rather than ask a member of staff to answer emails, ask them to be the person in charge of making the customer feel amazing. The language you use feeds into the culture of being the best at customer care. Don't expect your team to read your mind; instead sell them the vision and work out where they can fit in best with that vision.

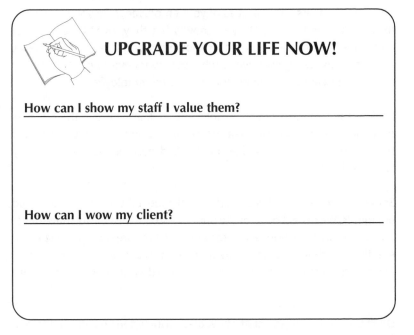

UPGRADE YOUR LIFE NOW!

How can I show my staff I value them?

How can I wow my client?

Office environment = office culture

Your office environment contributes to your office culture. Think about your workplace, and be honest here, what kind of culture does it feed into? Is it inspiring? Is it bland? Some of the largest corporations in the world offer tours of their HQs. If you can, take one of these tours and I guarantee it will change your perspective of how an office place should look. It will also make you understand how certain types of office environments can help employees. Touring the Facebook HQ in San Francisco was nothing short of inspiring. Could a visitor to your office say the same thing? You don't need a massive budget to start implementing a positive vibe throughout your workplace, and I'm certainly not suggesting that you suddenly adopt an uber-casual approach to your environment and start installing seats of the bean bag kind as opposed to those of the swivel kind. What I'm talking about here are simple but effective changes. Take a look at your office walls. What's on them? Unless you're working in an art gallery, pretentious artwork is of no benefit in a workplace. I'm sure it's beautiful but is it inspiring? Is it helping your employees generate ideas? If I were in charge of an open plan office, the first thing I would do is have one wall turned into a giant mood board, filled with positive statements, photos of employees enjoying themselves on staff retreats, anything that has an element of positivity attached to it.

Your meeting rooms should encourage creativity not hinder it, yet if you look at most standard conference rooms, you will find they lack imagination and stifle the production of ideas. When I set up my gym, I deliberately went against the stereotypical gym appearance. On the large wall in the reception area, I had a very talented graffiti artist create a vibrant image that reflected the upbeat energy of the business. My favourite positive statements were also painted in different areas around the gym itself. There was nothing cold or clinical about my gym and I firmly believe that helped contribute to the culture of the business.

When implementing new positive changes in your office, don't forget to do the same with your website. It should be renovated with the same level of care as you would the office. This is the first port of call for your customers, so pay close attention to the image it's portraying. Does your website have bio images of your employees or management members? If you are running a small business, this would be advisable as it immediately gives the customer the impression that your staff are warm and approachable.

Team goal-setting

Once a year take your team away for two days. This will be the annual team break. During that time away, incorporate an element of skill development, brainstorm ideas for customer initiatives, set goals for the coming 6–12 months and most importantly of all, revisit the vision of your company. The purpose of this is to have everyone working from the same page. For maximum impact, break down the goal-setting process into the areas of most importance and for each one commit to five goals that you will have executed by the following September. Don't just list them. Write down the key step you will endeavour to adopt for each one.

I'd like to point out here that you don't have to be an entrepreneur or a business owner to benefit from this section. The information applies to any kind of group, whether it be clubs, charities, community groups, volunteer groups, or whatever.

If, on the other hand, you are reading this to acquire development lessons in your personal life rather than your business life, you can still benefit. Instead I would suggest you take one day away for yourself where you can work on your goals for the next 6–12 months. I may use business as an example, but all the lessons here can be implemented right across the board.

Here's an example of a goal master plan set by a restaurant:

Area: Social media marketing
Goal 1 – Build up the email database to 20,000
Key step – When running a competition on our website, we will start using an app called Gleam so that those who wish to enter the competition will have to leave their email address as well as like our Facebook and Instagram accounts.
Goal 2 – Utilize the medium of Snapchat
Key step – Once a month, invite a blogger to the restaurant and have them Snapchat their experience.

Goal 3 – Utilize Instagram in a more productive way that will encourage new customers

Key step – Start photographing the most visually appealing dishes. Encourage people to tag the restaurant and share their own meal pictures on Instagram by offering a small prize, such as a voucher or a discount, to the person with the best shot.

Goal 4 – Start a YouTube channel

Key step – Have the head chef give a brief tutorial on how to make a Michelin star type dessert, a tasty breakfast smoothie, perfect pancakes, etc.

Goal 5 – Reach 50,000 followers on Facebook

Key step - Run a competition twice a month on Facebook. Entrants must share the page and tag at least two friends in the comment box. Prizes could include a hamper of food, meal for two, case of wine, etc.

Goal-setting retreats are great for motivating the team and firing up the enthusiasm. The hard part, however, is maintaining it. Annual retreats are a complete waste of time if you are not going to help your team stay on track during those 12 months. The day-to-day running of a business can easily side-track your employees from the bigger picture. The best way to keep them from losing sight of the annual goals is to have quarterly one-day retreats in which you look back on your progress since the annual meeting and figure out where improvements can be made if needed. Brainstorm more ideas that will help the business reach the annual goals set by the team the previous September.

Wherever possible, accompany the goal with either a percentage sign or a currency sign so that you can identify whether it was hit or missed. When it comes to goals, there is no room for 'sort of'. You cannot 'sort of' hit a goal. You have to be this blunt with your goal-setting otherwise you will fall short each time.

By the end of the day retreat, each employee should have a clear idea of what they will be doing in the short term to help the company achieve its overall goals for the year.

It goes without saying that weekly meetings should not be overlooked. Regardless of how busy you are, you need to make time for a 30-minute meeting with your staff in which you can discuss as a team the various things that are going well and the things that require attention. Are there any problems arising that you can solve together? These weekly meetings will untangle any knots that are starting to form within the business and help you catch problems during the early stages. It's worth keeping in mind that these meetings should be held at a time when the energy levels of the staff are beginning to dip. In my experience, this usually happens around 11am or 3pm. A team meeting can help re-energize the group and motivate them over the slump.

PILLAR 3: CAREER, EDUCATION, AND FINANCE

If you want to increase your income, then you are going to have to increase the number of people you help and how good you are at helping them. Look at how you can add more value to the workplace.

The old way of thinking was that if you spend 20 years in a workplace, you deserve a pay increase every year just by merit of the fact that you have been there for so long. The new way of thinking is more along the lines of, 'unless you're making a difference, why *should* you get paid more?'

Ask yourself the question, how big is the problem I'm solving and how can I solve it better? Or better still, can I solve a bigger problem?

Whether you're self-employed or working for a company, the advice is still the same: The bigger the problem you can solve, the more money you're going to make. The more people you help, the more money you can make. The better you are at helping them, the more money you will make.

So how do you get better? The answer is simple. More education.

If you increase your depth of skills or knowledge, you stand apart from your competitors. You can be a personal trainer who knows how to get people fit, or you can be a personal trainer who has a degree in physio or who has an almost expert knowledge of nutrition because of all the books you have read and studied.

Answer the question 'how can I add more value to my current role or to my clients?' This is the question you should always be asking yourself. If you own a restaurant, can you give a free refill, or get to know the names of your regular customers?

Every day is a school day for me; I am always learning. When I'm in the car or exercising, you can be sure I'm listening to audio books. If I'm on a long flight, you'll more than likely find me reading (or re-reading, as is often the case) the autobiography of an entrepreneur whose footsteps I want to follow. I have always had a voracious appetite for books that chronicle the life stories of the most successful and inspirational people. I don't read these books to pass the time, I do it so I can learn from the subject's mistakes and apply their most effective working practices to my own professional situation. This is my education. I especially love the book *The Strangest Secret* by Earl Nightingale. I have read through those pages more times than I can remember. It was authored over a decade before I was born but its core messages still ring true today. In it Nightingale writes about things such as adding value, adopting a positive mind-set, and the importance of concentrating on what you want as opposed to what you don't want. It was the book that kick-started the self-help industry and one I think I will always be re-reading.

It's very telling that Earl Nightingale, back in 1976, was writing of the importance of adding value. Your income will always be in direct correlation to the number of people you help and how good you are at helping them. This is something that will never change.

When you look at how you can add value, ask yourself the following two questions:

1. How am I different?

Why should a customer go to you and not a rival? What sets you apart? When you add more value, when you do more than required, when you go out on a limb, straight away you are demonstrating to the clients/ customers that you are different and worthy of their business. If you run a garage, maybe you could offer a free car wash with every service? That's added value right there.

You need to formulate a concise plan as to what you can do to encourage people not only to bring business your way but also recommend you to others. Never discount the power of a positive word about your business. Social media can do a lot, but nothing will ever beat a personal recommendation.

2. Why should my clients/customers return to me?

Think about your last three clients/customers. What reason do they have to return to you? More to the point, what reason did you give them?

Now ask yourself, what can you do to further improve the experience of your next three clients/customers? If you're running a small enterprise and feel as though you can't compete with the big guys, then you're already admitting defeat. There are plenty of boutique businesses out there operating very successfully against the industry big guys. To ensure an individual brings business your way, there needs to be something in it for them. This is why loyalty cards are so effective. The customer's loyalty is quite literally rewarded.

Selling a feeling

What you are selling in business is a feeling. Always remember that! Whether you're in business or not, people will always remember how you made them feel. When I was running my fitness business on the beach, it wasn't weight loss per se that people wanted, it was the feeling that came with losing weight. People had this idea that if they lost weight, they would feel more confident and sexy. Instead I looked at ways in which these feelings could be brought about as early as possible in the process. I didn't want my clients to wait until they were two stone lighter before they started feeling confident in themselves. I wanted them to enjoy that experience right away. This is why my business grew. People loved the feeling that came with participating in my workout sessions.

My friends and I always love to meet up in a coffee shop in Galway City called 37 West. Even though there are a few hundred coffee shops in the city, it's the one we always go to, without fail. The manager Roxy and her staff are amazing at what they do. They see countless different faces each day, yet they still know the names of all their regulars and they always take the time out to chat to you about your day, even when they're rushed off their feet. The interaction is so personal that you always feel really appreciated as a customer . . . notice again how it always comes back to how an individual is made to feel?

Be honest with yourself. Do you make your customers feel really valued and appreciated?

I want you to complete the following exercise once a week and you will be amazed at what you can come up with. If you need inspiration, look at other businesses in your sector. What are they doing that's adding more value?

If you're an employee, don't be afraid to put in the extra work before you get paid extra for it. Likewise, if you're a business owner, don't be afraid to give away great quality information for free in a bid to help attract

UPGRADE YOUR LIFE NOW!

How can I improve the service I'm offering?

Week 1 –

Week 2 –

Week 3 –

Week 4 –

Week 5 –

Week 6 –

customers. Giving away free information is the catalyst that will help them like and trust you. It's natural to feel a reluctance to give anything away or free when you're trying to make a profit, but you need to have faith that it will pay off in the long run and that people are going to come back to you as paying customers.

As an example, most car dealerships will place ads in the newspaper. What if a dealership went one step further and gave free content online about car maintenance, or tips on what to look for in a new car, or better still, tips on how to negotiate a better price with a car salesman!

By giving away this information, you have proven your worth and value, so when they do want to buy, they are going to come to you.

Can you become a specialist or an authority in your field? Let's use the medical industry as an example. A doctor charges a set fee, but a surgeon charges 20 times that because he's a specialist in what he does. A brain surgeon meanwhile can pretty much name his price because he's as good as indispensable. So how can you become more indispensable, more specialist, and consequently more valuable? It all comes back to education. You don't need to embark upon a PhD course. Read books, attend the seminars, complete courses, listen to audio books and podcasts, just do whatever it takes to get the knowledge that will make you stand out and help you progress.

When I decided to set up my personal training business on the beach in Galway, I approached a variety of different restaurants and asked them if they would let me create healthy menus for them using food they already had, and in return feature my logo and picture on the menu itself. I would also be able to recommend the restaurants in question to my clients because naturally the menus would be guaranteed to be in keeping with their meal plans. Having a presence on the menus in these restaurants gave me a great degree of credibility. I also had my posters in health food shops advertising different supplements they were selling. I trained a local girl in PR for free, and in return she would write press releases and generate media coverage for me. You could say I was pretty resourceful, and it paid off too!

A girl who joined my class – Katie – told me that she had just moved back to Galway when she saw a write-up about me that my PR girl had arranged in the local newspaper. When she went for a bite to eat in a restaurant in town, she saw my face and logo on the menu. Some time afterwards, during a trip to the health food shop, she spotted my posters. When I first met her, she told me that she couldn't get away from me, so she figured she might as well go train with me! This is the same effect you need to aim for. You need to be the go-to person in your industry. If you establish an image of authority and a reputation to match, then people will view you as the only person to go to. If you're in a profession such as medicine, law, horticulture, agriculture, etc, then you could submit a weekly Q&A column to a local newspaper or answer questions on local radio. Maybe you could film YouTube videos delivering content that most people would find useful. Utilizing the various social media channels – Facebook, Instagram, Twitter, Snapchat, and LinkedIn – will contribute hugely to your image. It's about having a presence and maintaining it to such an extent that when people need someone in your profession, you are the first person they think of.

Who can you learn from? Who is the best in your industry? Who is the best in marketing?

A lot of people fear being an authority because they look at the leaders of the industry, be they local, national, or international, and think 'who am I to rival them?'

The next time you find yourself thinking along those lines, I want you to stop yourself even finishing the sentence. Establish your own unique slant on your area of expertise and stop waiting for permission to step up and become the new authority.

UPGRADE YOUR LIFE NOW!

In your town/city, are you the go-to person in your industry?

If not, who is?

Why are they the go-to person? What are they doing?

What steps can you take to have a stronger presence and become the go-to person?

People are all too conscious of what their industry peers think of them. Here's the thing. It doesn't matter what others think of you. What matters is what your customer thinks of you. As an example, let's say you're a chef in your own catering business and you decide to release a newsletter each week in which you offer tips on home entertaining as well as general advice pertaining to all things culinary. Suddenly you start envisioning what your industry peers will say and consequently you decide not to press ahead out of fear that your content will be judged negatively by these people.

This is a common reaction. No person with any ounce of pride would want their work mocked or criticized, but here are the questions you need to ask yourself. Will the content you are providing be of help to the potential customer? Will your content prove to them that you know what you are talking about and can help solve their problem? If so, then don't give a second thought to the potentially critical opinions of your peers. Remember, some people are all too willing to take down those who take action, so unless you trust the opinion of the person in question, worry little about the possibility that your efforts or your work might be criticized. Don't try to impress others in your industry; instead concentrate on educating the potential customers in the marketplace so that they start to see you as the go-to person in your field. It all comes back to confidence and self-belief.

The ideal customer

Every business owner needs to identify their ideal customer, i.e. an avatar. When I was designing my customer avatar for the fitness classes, I went into great detail and even gave this 'customer' a name so as to make it seem as real as possible.

The avatar for my fitness class is called Jane; she's 25–45; she's got young kids, is busy, and wants to be in shape as well as feel a part of something. I go on to craft a detailed description of my ideal customer so that when I go to write my marketing material, work on my website or draft ideas for my classes, I try to speak directly to that 'ideal customer'. I am conscious that she is a busy woman so I figure she will want classes that are short but effective, meals that are family friendly.

Take the time to figure out your ideal customer and then mould your marketing and packaging around that person so you are speaking to them and meeting their needs.

UPGRADE YOUR LIFE NOW!

Create an avatar of your ideal customer.

If you want to improve your skillset, it would be well worth your while having a look at the Coursera website, an education platform that works in conjunction with universities and organizations around the world to offer online courses in a vast array of subjects. Even the prestigious Wharton School of Business offer courses though this site. There is a fee involved for some of the courses, but the website also has a number of free courses available. This is a great resource that I would strongly recommend you to utilize as much as possible.

If you're a busy person, the last thing you're going to want to do is bury your head in books for hours on end. You don't have to. The best way for a busy person to educate themselves is to employ what is known as the compound effect.

The compound effect

'Success isn't overnight. It's when every day you get a little better than the day before. It all adds up.'

Dwayne 'The Rock' Johnson, actor, producer,
and semi-retired professional wrestler

When I held my classes on the beach, there were ladies in their early 70s doing push-ups like it was second nature. Onlookers were shocked. They couldn't believe what they were seeing, but there was no magic to it, it was just a matter of consistency, or 'the compound effect' to give it its proper name.

Small actions carried out consistently day after day lead to massive results over time. This goes for everything, from business to fitness. We all want the fastest route to the finish line, but it's the people working away consistently in the background who will enjoy success.

The term 'compound effect' sounds a little too scientific for my liking, which is why I prefer to call it '1% better each day'. When I ran the gym, and even today when I carry out private coaching, I encourage clients to try to be 1% better every day. Instead of watching an hour of television each day, try instead to read for an hour. Over the course of 12 months, you will have learned so much, and, if the material you are reading is inspirational and stimulating, you will probably find that your mind-set has considerably improved too.

'Success is the sum of small efforts – repeated day in, day out.'

Robert Collier, American self-help author

The killer of confidence is comparison. We often look at others in our field and feel as though they are making so much more progress than us. Everyone's grass looks greener. Right now I want you to stop focusing on what others are doing and start concentrating on how you can be 1% better each day.

If you implement everything you read in this book, then over the next six weeks you will have completed 126 action steps, 126 gratitude posts, 42 acknowledgements, 42 hours of study, 7 hours of meditation, and 35 hours of training. It might not seem like much day to day but think about the overall yield you will enjoy.

Let's look at it this way. If you're a car salesman and you study car sales for one hour each day, by the end of the year you will have completed nine 40-hour workweeks of sales training. Already you have the edge on your colleagues.

Likewise, if you're a personal trainer and you study lower back pain for a year, after 12 months you will undoubtedly be one of the most knowledgeable people in the country on all things related to lower back pain.

I cannot emphasize this enough, the *only* way to make more money is to add more value to what you can offer, and the way to add more value is to upgrade your skillset. This can only be done through one medium: self-education.

If you even attempt to allow your inner critic to convince you that you are not academic, I want you to go back and read Chapter 2 again!

Don't be afraid to be the dumbest person in the room. You're going to hit the glass ceiling very quickly if you're aiming to be the proverbial big fish in the small pond. Put yourself in positions where you are challenged by people such as your mastermind group members, peers, coaches, mentors, fellow course members, whoever it may be, try to lean in on the discomfort that comes with knowing you are not the smartest in the

UPGRADE YOUR LIFE NOW!

Make a list of 10 people, books and resources that can help you fast track your way to your goal.

1.

2.

3.

4.

5.

6.

7.

8.

9.

10.

room. If you feel like the dumbest person in the room, then that's the room you should be in. It's very easy to walk into a networking group where you are the highest achiever, but if you want to see considerable growth, then you need to be where you feel a little bit uncomfortable to a point where you are asking yourself, 'should I be in this room?' Being in the company of those who are more knowledgeable than you will stretch your perception of what normal is.

PILLAR 4 – ADVENTURE

'We are always getting ready to live but never living.'
Ralph Waldo Emerson, American essayist,
lecturer, and poet

Back when I was feeling a little bit lost and everything was going a million miles an hour, I decided to take a few days' rest, so I travelled over to London to visit my friend Dax Moy. As we were chatting, I opened up about how overwhelmed I was beginning to feel. He pointed out a few home truths that actually changed the course of my life. He reminded me of the things I said I would do 'when I've made it', and pointed out that now was the time to go and do those things. We've all 'made it' in some way. I realized he was right. I needed a new change of direction. First though, I needed a proper break. Once I sold up my gym, I bought a ticket and went inter-railing around Europe for six weeks. My gym business had been doing phenomenally well but I still don't have any regrets about selling it. If anything, I am even more adamant now that it was the best decision I ever made because I am much happier with the life and career I have today.

We build this illusion of the things we want to do one day in the future, but these are the things we should be doing now. Dax opened my eyes to that realization and now I hope I'm opening yours.

Since I sold the gym, I have travelled all around America, Europe, Nepal, Dubai, Africa, and South America. I have done everything from petting cheetahs and swimming with dolphins to walking on fire and riding hot air balloons . . . the experiences I enjoyed on my travels could probably fill another book.

I loved Italy and Slovenia, but Africa was especially incredible. While there I went on a safari. On a trip like that, you really appreciate being present in the moment. When most people visit a landmark, it's all about getting the photo for social media (I've been guilty of this myself) but sometimes it's nice to just appreciate the experience and be present in that moment.

I've done the clichéd things like skydiving and going on meditation retreats, but then there are other things that weren't so run-of-the-mill such as embarking on a bread-making course in an eco-village! That was an interesting Saturday!

You don't have to go beyond the borders of your own country in order to find new experiences. Think about it. It's so easy to just waste away a weekend. Reclaim your weekends by seeking out new things to do. Travel to a part of the country you have never been to before. Search for unusual events that are taking place in your nearest city. Whatever you do, just get out of your comfort zone and, if you can, start ticking things off the bucket list before it gets rusty.

On my list, some of the things I want to do include:

- Go to one of Europe's biggest music festivals,
- Go scuba diving,
- Go a month without the internet,
- Meet and work with Oprah,
- Go on a surfing holiday,
- Attend the Summer Olympics,
- Drive a Ferrari,
- Attend Oktoberfest in Germany.

 UPGRADE YOUR LIFE NOW!

This is a fun 90-second exercise that I believe everyone should carry out at some point. The only requirement is that when answering the four questions, you have to think big and not allow yourself to limit your scope of possibility in any way. Give yourself 90 seconds per question and answer each one as if money were no object or if your current circumstances didn't dictate your plans.

1. What countries, places, or landmarks would you like to visit?
2. What experiences would you like to have? *Example: hot air balloon ride/eat in a Michelin Star restaurant/scuba diving/spend a night in the Icehotel, etc.*
3. What would you like to own? *Example: holiday home/pair of Jimmy Choo heels, etc.*
4. What would you like to learn? *Example: tap dance/play an instrument/new language, etc.*

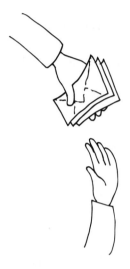

PILLAR 5 – CONTRIBUTION

'Regardless of where you are in life, you are in a position to help other people.'

Colm Divilly, my dad!

My dad always drilled it into me that regardless of where I was in life, I was in a position to help other people. I've been able to avail of some amazing opportunities, but I've always found that I got the most fulfilment from my contribution work.

Contribution can range anywhere from doing something in your local community, to checking in on someone who hasn't been enjoying the best of health. I used to think that you had to have achieved a certain level of celebrity or wealth before you could contribute effectively, but now I realize that anyone can change the world in their own way, and I firmly believe that everyone should *want* to contribute and make a change not least because of the level of fulfilment they will get from doing so.

'Contribution leads to an increased connection with other people.'
Pat Divilly

In my experience, it's a good idea to uncover your 'why' before you begin the contribution. Your 'why' will play a big part in the effort you will invest in contributing.

Throwing money into a fundraising bucket is perfectly fine, but you will enjoy much more fulfilment if you decide on a cause that is close to your heart and matters most to you and your family.

The stronger the 'why', the more likely you are to make the contribution and carry out the work required.

 UPGRADE YOUR LIFE NOW!

Think of one thing that has affected you and your family either directly or indirectly.

What cause relates to this? _____

What can you do to help this cause? _____

UPGRADE YOUR LIFE

If you are struggling with this exercise, here's an example:

1. Think of one thing that has affected you and your family either directly or indirectly?
   A neighbour of mine was a victim of domestic violence.
2. What cause relates to this?
   In the city, there is a shelter for women and children.
3. What can you do to help this cause?
   I will donate food, toys, and clothes to the shelter. I will round up my family members to do a clear-out of their wardrobes and kids' playrooms so that we can donate clothes and toys to the shelter.

Project impact

I used to tell myself that some day I would start a charity but then it occurred to me that there was no point in waiting; that I should just do it right there and then. So I did! With the help of a group of friends, Project Impact was born.

I'm fortunate that I have a large social media following but I felt that I would be doing a great disservice to people if all I talked about was fitness and nutrition, so I set up an organization that allows me and those who donate to have more control over where the money goes and how it is spent. In recent times, question marks have been placed over the salaries being paid to charity CEOs. I always felt that every cent of every donation should go to the charity and not contribute to a massive CEO salary, so when Project Impact was established, we decided from the get-go that it would be all volunteer based.

Our aim is to help smaller charities raise awareness and funds, so the team and I carry out fundraisers for different foundations. We come in, help them raise as much money as possible, and then rock on to the next charity. It's the same premise as Secret Millionaire but from a charity perspective. Before we undertake a fundraiser, we carry out our homework so that we know exactly where the money will be going and what it will fund.

There's complete transparency, so those who donate know exactly where their money will be going, what it will be spent on, and how it will benefit the foundation.

We're just a group of ordinary people trying to make an extraordinary difference by giving smaller causes a loud voice. The charity is still in its infancy so we don't have a massive budget, but what we lack in finances we definitely make up for in determination.

It's like I said in the previous section – we are all in a position to give back. You don't have to take the big leap I took by setting up a charity, but if it's something you want to do, then go for it.

 Chapter 4 Cheat Sheet to Upgrade Your Life

- If you want to live a happy, fulfilling life, then there are five areas you must tend to: health, relationships, career/education/finance, adventure, and contribution. If you feeling discontented and unfulfilled, it is because you are neglecting one or more of these important elements.
- If you want to increase your profit, you need to increase the value you are offering to the customer. The best way to increase value is through self-education.
- If you want to build on your skills, look at the Coursera website. This is an education platform that works in conjunction with universities to offer a wide variety of free and paid-for online courses in many fields.

- Read books by entrepreneurs who have done what you want to do. Learn from their mistakes, and use their experiences in business as a template for your own journey.
- If you feel you are too busy to undertake a course or read books, then employ the compound effect. Remember small actions carried out consistently day after day lead to massive results over time. Also take a look back at Step 3 The Brakes in Chapter 3 for tips on better time management.

Upgrading My Life: Una Murphy (client)

One very effective tool I learned from Pat is the use of vision boards.

Based on a quote from one of Pat's favourite authors, Napoleon Hill, you can be confident that once you put something on your vision board, you already believe that you can achieve it, 'Whatever the mind can conceive and believe, it can achieve.'

When I put together my first vision board, I had been working in the same office job for almost thirty years. There were redundancies in the pipeline but not everyone who applied would get it. I put a picture of money on the board to represent the redundancy package that I was hoping to get. I also wanted to start doing mosaics, but at the time I had never done that craft before nor had I any background in art whatsoever. I was lucky enough to get into the New York Marathon and had a picture of the time I wanted to achieve on the board (I also had it on my marathon training plan to keep me focused). Daniel Craig was starring in a sold-out Broadway play the weekend I was going to be in New York, but several attempts to get tickets had failed. By fixing these goals in my mind through the vision board I was able to work towards them. None were achieved overnight, but by moving forward and trying to make them happen they all did.

I ran the New York Marathon in 3:55:37 and got my qualifying time for the Boston Marathon, which was the goal.

I sat very contentedly in the fifth row at the Daniel Craig play the day before the marathon and enjoyed every minute!

I got my redundancy from the office job, which included a training grant to go on a mosaic mural workshop in Mexico and it was an amazing experience.

I have been on several more mosaic workshops since then and have covered two of my garden walls with mosaics and am currently involved with a community art project to mosaic the garden wall for a local group.

There's a quote I love that really sums up the benefit of goal-setting. It goes 'set your mind on a definite goal and observe how quickly the world stands aside to let you pass'.

CHAPTER 5

WHAT SUCCESSFUL PEOPLE DO

'There's not much difference between a fantasist and a visionary. We all have dreams and without dreams in business, I don't believe you can be successful. The trick is to turn them into reality.'
— Theo Paphitis, British retail entrepreneur

The ideal daily routine for peak performance in life and business

The first thing you need to realize is that ALL high performers look after their bodies. That's *why* they are high performers. They understand that unless they look after themselves, they can't perform to the best of their ability, whether it be in their career or their personal life. You've read about the five pillars, now you are going to read about how the most successful people incorporate the various practices into their daily routines, and most importantly, how you can too.

Get active (exercise)

(Recommended time: minimum 30 minutes)
There's no denying the direct correlation between fitness and high performance in the workplace. If you examine the world's leaders in

business, politics, entertainment, and so on, you will find that each of them carries out some form of daily exercise lasting between 45 minutes to over an hour. I would recommend a minimum of 30 minutes. Every morning President Barack Obama wakes up an hour earlier than scheduled so he can exercise for 45 minutes. Twitter co-founder Jack Dorsey wakes at 5.30am to meditate and go for a six-mile jog. Mark Cuban likewise always makes a point of working out in his gym for an hour. Bill Gates on the other hand likes to multi-task. He pounds the treadmill for an hour each morning while watching courses from the Teaching Company. PayPal co-founder Max Levchin rises at 5am to go cycling, and I'm not talking about a relaxing bike ride either. This guy all but burns the tyres off his bike!

In my opinion, it's worth developing a balance between exercises of a vigorous nature and ones that perhaps have a slightly more relaxing vibe about them. Maybe three days out of the seven you could do some yoga or go for a brisk walk. These are brilliantly restorative. Personally, when I need to de-stress, I hit the swimming pool. Until I decided to learn how to swim, however, weight training was always my go-to activity whenever I needed to wind down after a long day. Maybe you would prefer venting your stress on a kick-boxing bag or a rowing machine?

Whatever your preference, it's important that the activity you choose is one you enjoy. Contrary to popular belief, an effective exercise regime does not have to be torturous or involve running 10 or 20 miles, unless of course you want it to. You can still become very fit without having to do that. It's not about killing yourself on the treadmill, it's about incorporating some active movement into your daily routine. Everyone is incredibly busy these days so establish something that works for you. If you have a meeting scheduled with another person, does it have to take place in a boardroom? Could you go for a walk with that person and have the meeting that way? This might sound crazy, but it's not uncommon. SoulCycle bosses often carry out meetings in a SoulCycle class; Facebook's Mark Zuckerberg has been known to conduct business dealings while out walking. I also recently read that more and more Wall Street figures have taken to the new trend of carrying out meetings with their clients over a gym barbell as opposed to over a restaurant bar. If you're worried that inviting a client out for a brisk walk might sound daft, just remember, they will probably appreciate the opportunity to get some fresh air and gentle exercise themselves.

Embrace the calm (meditation)

(Recommended time: minimum of 10 minutes)
'Meditation more than anything in my life was the biggest ingredient of whatever success I've had.'

> *Ray Dalio, billionaire and founder of the world's*
> *largest hedge fund firm, Bridgewater Associates*

I recently set up a Facebook group called '40 Days of Meditation'. An interactive group like this will help give you such focus plus it's also an excellent form of motivation because you can see the different ways in which it is benefiting others in the group. I remember one lady who wrote about the calming impact the meditation was having on her young child who had Down's syndrome. She explained that he would become quite unsettled at times, but once they started meditating together, it put him at ease and helped calm him down immensely.

It's ironic that we often place little value on things that are free but do so much for us, preferring instead to place value on things that are expensive and do so little for our welfare. Meditation is free, doesn't require anything other than your time, and yet it is one of the most beneficial things you can do for yourself. Remember, if a car can't slow down, it's going to crash. Simple as. It's the very same with our minds and bodies. Most people don't know how to slow down and embrace the calm, which is why we consequently crash and burn. It is so important that you incorporate 10 minutes of meditation into your day. If you introduce it into your daily routine for the next six weeks, I promise you will be astonished by the difference. You will be more productive and creative, and far more equipped to deal with problems, pressure, and stress, not to mention enjoy heightened clarity and improved cognitive functioning. Meditation strengthens your resilience and, as I already explained in the last chapter, makes you more bullet-proof in stressful situations.

It's no surprise to learn that some of the world's top companies have begun offering meditation classes for their employees. After all, stress and anxiety impact significantly on performance, but they can also affect a person's perspective, thus resulting in them mishandling a problematic situation. Meditation, however, helps you adopt a calmer approach when the stress hits.

Meditation and mindfulness also help to build an inner environment conducive to the creation of ideas. Have a problem that you can't figure out the answer to? Meditate on it! It's what most leaders do. If you feel you don't have time to meditate for 10 minutes each day, then it's a sign that you actually *need* 30 minutes of meditation. Remember, if you have time to check Facebook, Snapchat, Instagram, and Twitter, you have time to sit in stillness. No excuses!

 Regardless of whether you're a meditation novice or a pro, check out my guided meditation track at www. upgradeyourlifebook.com.

Show gratitude

(Recommended: three things daily)
Don't be deceived by the simplicity of this task. Trust me, its impact is huge. All you have to do each morning and/or night is list five things you are grateful for. You can close your eyes and think them through, type them into your tablet or phone, or write them down in a notebook, i.e. a gratitude journal. Personally, I find the latter to be far more effective.

I promise you, this is not some new-age notion. By concentrating on the things you should be grateful for, you are rewiring your brain to pay attention to the positive more than the negative. Practising this over time means you will find yourself less fazed by bad days. If you only have time to perform the ritual once a day, then I would recommend doing it at night before bed. By focusing on the good things that happened throughout your day, you are reducing the effects the bad moments have on your subconscious. This will even result in you enjoying a better quality of sleep because your brain is tuned to the positive, rather than the negative.

Leading CEOs and business figures have all witnessed the benefits of practising daily gratitude—so much so that many have introduced the ritual into the workplace.

It really does contribute to a productive day because it places you in a positive abundance-welcoming mind-set, as opposed to one of scarcity. People with a scarcity mind-set always concentrate on what they *don't* have, and are consequently never in a position to attract better things into their lives. I want you to flip this on its head and look at what you *do* have. Even if you have had the worst day known to man, force yourself to look for the positive moments that occurred throughout. Maybe the bad day made you tougher? There's good to be found in everything. It's just a matter of rewiring your brain to immediately see and appreciate the good in every situation. Whether you believe in it or not, practising a daily gratitude ritual will improve your sense of happiness, your self-esteem, and your mental strength, as well as contribute to the reduction of aggression, anxiety, and depression.

Ideally, you should complete a gratitude list twice a day.

Every morning, I like to take between two and five minutes to jot down as many things as possible for which I am grateful. This puts me in a positive mind-frame before I have even left the house. The list often includes things like . . . having a job I love, living by the sea in one of the most scenic places in Ireland, being able to help people change their lives for the better, etc. Then at night before I go to bed, I write down five things that happened that day that I am grateful for.

Gayle Karen Young, former Chief Talent and Culture Officer of the Wikimedia Foundation, once wrote: 'To not be grateful is to not see that we are gifted with bodies that breathe to experience this life.' I can 100% relate to this. One thing I am eternally grateful for is having a healthy state of mind. As you know from the first chapter, I have experienced dark days just like everyone else, so now when I look back on that time, I am eternally grateful I came through it with a profound appreciation for my mental health. This is why I also like to carry out as much charity work as possible for the depression awareness group, Console. Don't just write anything on the list for the sake of filling it out. Really think about what you are grateful for in your life.

Andrew Yang, CEO of Venture for America, uses his phone to record three things he is grateful for. These lists, he says, have a positive impact on his mind-set whenever he looks back on them. Billionaire businessman John Paul DeJoria also takes five minutes each morning to think of specific things for which he is thankful for in his life.

Facebook COO Sheryl Sandberg used the gratitude ritual to help her regain some sense of joy and happiness following the tragic death of her husband, Dave Goldberg. When she felt 'overwhelmed with just getting through each day', Adam Grant, her friend and a professor at Wharton University, advised her to write down three things she did well, regardless of how small or insignificant the accomplishments seemed. It worked wonders, so much so that for 2016, she resolved to start writing down three joyful moments that occurred in her life each day, and to 'try to focus on finding joy in the mundane and the profound'.

A younger me would have dismissed gratitude journaling as an airy fairy practice that carried little merit, but that was before I knew first hand just how beneficial it could be. Don't discredit this practice until you have tried it for yourself. Entrepreneur Gary Vaynerchuk says his daily ritual of practising gratitude carried him through some of his toughest moments in business, so if it works this well for people in seriously high-pressured environments, then why wouldn't it work wonders for you too?

For the next six weeks, I want you to use the success journal at the end of this book to document the different things you are grateful for. This will actively help you create a productive new habit.

Once you have honed this technique, I want you to concentrate on reaching the next level of gratitude, which involves finding the good in the bad. Let's take the breakup of a relationship as an example. When it happens, your initial reaction is to feel down and out, but if you start training your mind to focus on the aspect of gratitude in every situation then you can turn it on its head and instead recognize the positive element. Maybe you say to yourself, 'I'm grateful now that I have family and friends to support me at this time; I'm grateful that I now have more free time to spend how I wish without having to answer to anyone.'

This is a technique I employ all the time. In recent months, for example, I took on an overwhelming amount of work but rather than complain about the fact that I'm extremely busy and have no free time, I flip it on its head and instead voice my gratitude that so many people want to work with me. Prior to giving my TEDx talk, my nerves were so bad I didn't just have butterflies in my stomach, I had bats! Rather than let the anxiety get the better of me, however, I instead kept reminding myself that I was grateful to have been given such an amazing opportunity. I reframe the story in my head and view it from a different perspective.

If you don't think this technique will work for you in a stressful situation, then instead find a piece of music that will help reframe your thoughts for you. The world's youngest self-made billionaire, Spanx founder Sarah Blakely, isn't the biggest fan of giving talks, so rather than dwell on her thoughts before she goes on stage, she instead sticks on her earphones and listens to Eminem's song 'Sing for the Moment' to psych herself up and get rid of any nerves she may be feeling. She listens to the lyrics and embraces the moment rather than focusing on her dislike of public speaking. It all comes back to making the effort to reframe your thoughts until it starts to happen automatically. That's the power of gratitude journaling.

Acknowledge and compliment others

(Recommended: one each day to start)
In the space of three years, I went from having five clients on a beach to having 10,000 members signed up to my gym and online courses. I credit this progress to the simple habit of acknowledging people. Compliments, acknowledgements, and encouraging comments are an incredibly powerful tool to utilize in both your personal and professional lives. Do you remember the last time someone said something genuinely kind to you or encouraged you in a positive way? When was the last time you were sent a token of good will, such as a bouquet of flowers? Think about how good those types of gestures made you feel, or would make you feel. It doesn't happen nearly as often as it should, but think about how your life and mind-set would change if you were to do that for someone once a day? Even something as a simple as a daily compliment or an acknowledgement of someone's efforts would have an amazing impact on your life.

The idea behind this is reciprocity – what you put out there will come back. An acknowledgement can be a text to a loved one, a smile to a stranger, buying a coffee for a stranger, just one small thing every day that will make a positive difference to someone's life.

In one of my life-coaching seminars, I had my group carry out an exercise that involved them putting ten 5 cent coins in one pocket, and for every compliment they gave someone, they had to transfer one coin over to the other pocket. It's cheesy, but it creates awareness and it works. Don't feel bad if you haven't already been acknowledging people every day, you just weren't aware of it. Now that it's been brought to your attention, you have a good reason to start.

Businessman Mark Cuban often talks about the importance of 're-earning his business every day'. He may have amassed a colossal fortune but that doesn't mean he takes this success for granted. Cuban is only too aware of the young guns coming up behind him and so, to ensure he stays ahead of the game, he approaches each day looking for ways to 're-earn his business'.

Ask yourself every morning, what am I going to do today that will make someone else's day better? What would make someone smile? Whether it's something as simple as a text to a loved one at night, or something more elaborate like a surprise bouquet of flowers to a client to thank them for their business, ask yourself what way you could show your appreciation to someone?

 ## UPGRADE YOUR LIFE NOW!

List five people who deserve an acknowledgement from you, followed by the way in which you would do it.

1.

2.

3.

4.

5.

Educate yourself

(Recommended: At least 60 minutes of study each day, e.g. reading, listening to audiobooks and podcasts, etc)
The wealthiest, most successful people never stop learning. I'm not talking about doctorates and degrees. I'm talking about information in specific fields that is of benefit to them. It may be a book on self-improvement or a podcast relating to the industry they operate in – either way, they soak up all the knowledge they can. You could say they operate by the theory that they are what they read. Entrepreneur Steve Siebold authored the book *How Rich People Think* after studying more than 1,200 of the world's wealthiest people over the course of three decades. He found that they placed more emphasis on lifelong learning and acquisition of knowledge, as opposed to formal education.

This is not unlike what Napoleon Hill discovered when writing *Think and Grow Rich*. This is one of my all-time favourite books, and one I have re-read over and over since I was a teenager.

> 'Successful men, in all callings, never stop acquiring specialised knowledge related to their major purpose, business, or profession. Those who are not successful usually make the mistake of believing the knowledge-acquiring period ends when one finishes school.'
>
> *Napoleon Hill, Think and Grow Rich*

It's no coincidence that some of the world's most successful business figures happen to have a crazy appetite for reading. Self-made Atlanta businessman J.B. Fuqua built a multibillion-dollar conglomerate during his lifetime, but while his formal education may have stopped once he left high school, his desire to learn did not. He regularly borrowed books from the library in the local Duke University, all of which helped him become a business powerhouse. Once he started to achieve financial success, he expressed his gratitude to the university by becoming their biggest benefactor.

The average morning for a lot of hugely successful business figures always incorporates some form of reading routine. Former president of Google Enterprise Dave Girouard reads the *New York Times*, the *Wall Street Journal*, followed by a book on Winston Churchill's best speeches. Starbucks CEO Howard Schultz wakes at 5am to enjoy a coffee while he reads the *Seattle Times*, the *Wall Street Journal*, and the *New York Times*. He has maintained his morning reading routine for over 20 years. BuzzFeed founder Jonah Peretti devours the business section of the *New York Times* each morning during his commute to work. Fast food chain CEO Cheryl Bachelder likes to focus her morning reading material on the subject of leadership and has even cited this routine as being one of the most important parts of her day.

 If for one year, you were to study for an hour each day, it would add up to nine 40-hour work weeks. This is a prime example of the compound effect.

So how are you improving in your business and personal life? In business, if you are not learning more about your field, then how can you be the best in it? If you don't have time, multi-task. Listen to a podcast when exercising. I turned my car into a mobile classroom just by listening to audiobooks every time I drive somewhere.

Regardless of how busy you are, there is always time to learn if you employ the art of multi-tasking. Most CEOs listen to audiobooks while they exercise or commute (remember Bill Gates' routine?). There are several pockets of time throughout the day that you can devote to learning. Some days you might only have time to read a *Forbes* article, other days you may have time to read a couple of chapters from a book (hopefully this one!). It doesn't matter how much you learn, what matters is that you are learning and strengthening your mind. Whether you want to improve in business, learn a new language, or grow your skillset when it comes to hobbies, always remember the compound effect I spoke about in the last chapter. As long as you are striving to improve by 1% each day, it will all add up.

Take up journaling

As part of this education step, I want you to take up journaling. Sometimes people study so much that they place all their faith in the advice of others rather than trying to listen to their own gut feeling and institution. It's important to study but it's equally as important to have self-belief and confidence in your own decisions. The purpose of journaling is to encourage you to explore different questions, thoughts, and ideas.

To get you started, I have below listed 30 journaling questions for you to answer in whatever order you wish. As you can see, one of the questions is: 'What would you achieve in your life if you overcame your current fears?' If you wrote about that subject for one hour, you would learn more about yourself from that one question alone than you would from any book. Reading books is a form of external study because you are absorbing what someone else is thinking. Journaling on the other hand is a form of internal study, and its benefits lie in its power to reveal things about the writer that even the writer was unaware of.

It's so important to focus on creation rather than consumption. Consumption is taking on reality TV, other people's content and ideas, buying things to fill a void. Consumption is necessary to a point but it needs to be balanced out with creation. Journaling is a very effective form of creation.

The next time you study a book, step away from it and take some breathing space. Then take some time to journal about what you learned from the book and what it meant to you. Ten people could read the same book and have 100 different perspectives on the messages contained within it. By journaling, you are figuring out how best to apply what you learned from the book to different areas of your own life. Journaling about a book, a course, a podcast, etc, will help you figure out how it can best help you.

UPGRADE YOUR LIFE NOW!

1. How do you want to be remembered?

2. What legacy would you like to leave behind?

3. What will you miss out on in life if you hold on to your current fears?

4. What would you achieve in your life if you overcame your current fears?

5. What would you go after in life if you knew you couldn't fail?

6. What's working/not working in your business/workplace right now?

7. What's working not working in your relationships at the moment?

8. What would you do if you had more time?

9. What would you do if you had more money?

10. What is the one change you could make right now to upgrade your life and what could it help?

11. What do you want?

12. Who do you love?

13. What people, places, and experiences fill you with energy and good vibes?

14. What is the next step you need to take toward your biggest goal?

15. How could you help more people reach their goals?

16. What is the next step you could take toward improving your relationships?

17. What were the happiest moments and days of your life?

18. List at least 50 things that make you feel good.

19. What does success mean to you?

20. What does a fulfilled life look like to you?

21. What advice would you give your 18-year-old self?

22. If you could change one thing about your current life what would it be?

23. What would your perfect day look like?

24. What are the qualities you look for in a friend?

25. Where will you be five years from now?

26. If today was your last day what would you do?

27. If you could start your life over and re-write your script what would you do differently?

28. If you could ask a genie for one wish what would it be?

29. What are the biggest life lessons you have learnt thus far?

30. If you had enough money to never work again what would you do?

Focus your action steps

(Recommended: at least three each evening/night)
In my own group The Upgrade Academy (www.upgradeyourlifebook. com), we keep one another accountable with a daily 'accountability log' where everyone checks in once they have completed their three highest priority tasks.

Rather than jotting down every meaningless task that needs to be completed that day, write down your top three to five priority tasks, and concentrate on these.

This is an effective form of time management and helps keep you focused on what's urgent or important. From tonight onwards, I want you to start listing your three highest priority tasks that must be completed the following day. This way, your subconscious can think about it while you sleep.

Maybe your list will go something like this:

Tomorrow I will . . .
Make five sales calls
Email each staff member with a date and time for the group meeting
Devote 30 minutes to reading a new book

When you wake up, you immediately know what needs to be done. You feel more organized because you have given a sense of clarity to the highest priority tasks for the day ahead.

This daily ritual is one followed by Kenneth Chenault, the CEO of American Express. Before leaving the office each evening, Chenault writes down the top three tasks he wants to accomplish the following day. This simple task helps him feel on top of things and gives him a head start on a day that hasn't even yet begun. I would safely bet that over 95% of high achievers carry out this routine each night.

Remember, the antidote to fear is action

Fear is what holds us back from doing the things we want to do in different areas and the antidote to that is action. Action alleviates anxiety.

People ask me how I get so much done. It's simple. I just *do* stuff. People overthink things, try to get things perfect before they start, but this can be overwhelming. Sometimes it helps not to think too much about something and to just do it.

Action is also the antidote to procrastination.

Management consultant David Allen has a great tip for beating procrastination. It's called the two-minute rule. Start with a task that can be carried out in two minutes or less. If it's a big task, then break it down and get to work on the part of it that requires only two minutes. Why is this effective? Because it's easy to continue once you start. Getting started is always the hardest part.

Stop looking for perfect and stop looking for permission

You need to realize the true cost of fear and once you do, you will understand why it is so important to overcome it. The cost of fear is living a life that is NOT the one you want. It's NOT having the relationships or the career you want; NOT having the voice you want; NOT being able to show up as your true self. It's like having to wear a mask all the time. While fear holds us back from our plans, procrastination is what kills and buries them. Don't be one of those people who always waits until circumstances are just right, take action now and mould your circumstances to suit your plans. Don't wait for permission to be good enough to step up and write a book, start a blog, carry out a public speaking engagement, ask for a promotion, or whatever it may be. Too many people stand back and watch other people making progress and transforming their ideas into reality. Too many live in fear. Being a leader means showing other people what is possible by doing the things yourself. Going from being a spectator in life to being a participant. Your superiors are not going to take you aside one day and tell you it's time to take over, so stop waiting for perfection and permission, and step up as a leader in your own life.

'The opposite of courage is conformity.'

Earl Nightingale, American radio
personality and author

The importance of establishing a morning routine

I have already spoken about the ways in which various successful business figures incorporate different practices into their daily routines – things like meditation, exercise, reading, and gratitude – but did you notice that most of them opt to carry out these rituals as part of their morning routine? Every high achiever I have met or interviewed for my podcast series has established an effective morning routine. The logic behind it is simple. When you take control of your morning, you take control of the day. You will also find that most successful individuals are early risers. Waking early enables them to make a productive head start on the day. As a result, they feel more in control and organized.

If everyone adopted this approach, we would move mountains.

Unfortunately, the reality is that most people have a routine that only involves checking their phone before they have even rolled out of bed. It's a habit, but it's not a good one. Most of us are reactive to what's going on in the world before we have even had time to think about our own well-being. Another common morning scenario involves the post-snooze-button-drama. We postpone getting up until the very last minute, and consequently we end up running late and grabbing breakfast on the go.

Sometimes, breakfast isn't even an option. That, combined with rising stress levels, is not the ideal start to a productive day.

I remember reading an article in which a high ranking army officer stated that the one thing people should do every morning to set themselves up for the day is to take the time to make their bed neatly. This, he said, would give them a sense of organization and a clear mind-set. It sounds like common sense, but for most people, morning time is nothing more than a mad rush.

Your morning routine should ideally include some exercise, meditation and entries in your gratitude list, but you need to find something that's practical for you. Maybe you can only fit in 10 minutes of exercise, five minutes of meditation, and a few lines in the gratitude journal. If that's all you can do, then that's all you can do. It's better than doing nothing, and trust me, it does make a difference.

 How to form a better morning routine

1. Plan a good breakfast the night before. Something like a smoothie bowl or overnight oats are always good options because they can be made in advance and are so tasty and nutritious. Try to plan a breakfast that you can look forward to enjoying.

   On my website (www.upgradeyourlifebook.com) you will find a number of breakfast recipes that were created to give you the best energy kick start to the day.
2. Turn off all phone notifications an hour before you go to sleep. You need to allow your body time to wind down. This will enable you to enjoy a more peaceful night's sleep.

3. When you wake, drink a pint of water. There are so many health benefits to drinking water on an empty stomach upon wakening. Not only will it fire up your metabolism, it also aids mental clarity.

4. When forming the habit of an effective morning routine, try to maintain it at weekends too, particularly at the beginning. You want the habit to stick. By continuing this routine through the weekend, you will find your energy levels are more consistent. By getting up at 6am during the week and 10am during the weekend, those Monday mornings will be even harder!

5. Don't hit the snooze button in the morning. The temptation is hard to resist, but falling back to sleep again will only make you sluggish and tired when you do get up.

6. Find a book you know you will love, ideally one that will encourage a positive mind-set, then sit in quietness for 15 minutes with a cup of coffee or a smoothie and read a chapter. This is a great way to calm the mind and prepare you for the busy day ahead.

Carrying out these tasks each morning will set you up nicely for the day. In fact, once you introduce an effective strategy to your morning, you should also find that you are far more productive than usual.

Remember what I said in the last chapter about following the example set by the high achievers?

Well here's how the most successful business figures spend their mornings:

Cal Newport: The renowned computer academic and author starts each morning by taking his dog for a walk, usually while listening to an audiobook. He even stops by the local playground to do some pull-ups. He finds the solitude helps him produce interesting ideas. When he returns home following the walk, he allocates half an hour to household tasks such as paying bills, etc. This routine helps him stay organized and allows for the rest of the day to flow smoothly.

Steve Reinemund: The former CEO of Pepsi goes for a four-mile run at 5am. This is followed by prayer/meditation, reading the newspapers, and breakfast with his family.

John Paul DeJoria: The billionaire tycoon kick starts his day with five to 10 minutes of silence. He once told an interviewer that he tries to be as 'present as possible' by lying in silence for five minutes from the moment he wakes up. Next, he checks his calendar for the day and follows up with assistants. He also follows the golden rule of 'eating the live frog first' by starting his day with the most pressing tasks such as important phone calls.

Michelle Gass: The Starbucks president rises at 4.30am to go for a run and enjoy some quiet time before work. She has openly credited her morning routine with having increased her happiness and productivity.

Brad Lande: If you're more of a night owl than an early bird, don't fret. BirchBox Man founder Brad Lande was not a morning person either, until, that is, he trained himself to be. By introducing certain habits into his routine, he is reaping the benefits of being a fully-fledged member of the early bird family. He starts his morning with a cup of hot water and lemon. This is followed by meditation, yoga, and a breakfast smoothie. As he said himself, he shifted his mornings from being 'a sleepy blur to a clear awakening'.

Now, before you move on to the next chapter have you completed the success rituals and core value exercises? If not, why are you reading on?

UPGRADE YOUR LIFE NOW!

Describe your average morning, from the time you wake up to the time you arrive at work:

Now, taking inspiration from some of the examples I have given you, write down your ideal morning routine here for the same timeframe:

 Chapter 5 Cheat Sheet to Upgrade Your Life

- If you want to be a high performer you need to take immense care of your mind and body. If you study all the great success stories in business and life, you will find that they all look after their bodies. That's *why* they are high performers.
- Each night, write down three top priority tasks for the following day. This will give you a head start on the day.
- The antidote to fear is action so stop looking for perfect and stop looking for permission, just go for it.
- Fatigued and unproductive? Establish an effective morning routine and those problems will pretty much disappear.
- Whether you choose to read a book, undergo a course, or listen to podcasts and audio books, educate yourself as much as

possible so that you become an expert in your industry. If you are not learning more about your field, then how can you be the best in it?

- Like exercise, meditation is another daily ritual carried out by successful people. Do you think it's a coincidence that the majority of high achievers rave about the benefits of meditation? Meditation will help optimize your performance. If you don't believe me, try it for the six weeks and see for yourself!

CHAPTER 6

THE SUCCESS JOURNAL

'The act of writing is the act of discovering what you believe.'

—Sir David Hare, dramatist

Throughout the book I have given you the tools to help you quite literally change your life. Knowing them is no good unless you plan on implementing them and the best way to do this is to turn them into habits. The success journal is the opportunity to do just that. As I said at the start of the book, none of these rituals will work in isolation. It's simply not enough to implement just one guideline, you have to implement them all. The exercises throughout the book will have helped shape your internal dialogue. The success journal is now going to help you carry out the all-important external actions.

Assuming you will have completed the exercises outlined in the book so far, you will have:

Set your intention
Established 10 things that equate to success for you
Listed your core values
Outlined the kind of life you want to live
Highlighted your empowering stories
Reframed your disempowering stories

Completed your 'I Am' statement
Set your goals
Identified the brakes
Established the resources that will help you accelerate your learning
Outlined the ways in which you can implement the wow factor
Created an avatar of your ideal client
Listed the books/resources that will help you fast track your goal
Begun journaling by answering the questions listed
Creatively answered the four '90-second questions'
Established your ideal morning routine.

There's a lot to remember, so this journal will keep you right on track for the next six weeks, by the end of which it will be second nature. The first week is the hardest, but if you work through it, I promise you that within the six-week timeframe, you WILL start to see results. Just think, in only six weeks' time you will be a new person, more energized and productive and on your way to an incredibly fulfilled life.

 If you need additional support from those who are also undertaking this new major life change, feel free to join my Facebook group, 'Upgrade Your Life'. You can find the link on www.upgradeyourlifebook.com.

If you are a little unsure of how to complete the different sections in the journal, here's an excerpt from my success journal that you can use as a guide:

Get Active (30–45 minutes) 40-minute swimming lesson, covered 1.5km
Meditation Embrace the Calm (10–15 minutes) 10-minute guided meditation from www.upgradeyourlifebook.com
Education (60 minutes) 60-minute podcast whilst commuting
Acknowledgement Sent flowers to a client who has been with me for six months

Gratitude:
1. Grateful for coffee
2. Grateful to my best friend for keeping me accountable at swimming
3. Grateful for a new business opportunity

Action Steps
1. Post a webinar for potential clients
2. Write a blog post
3. Make five sales calls

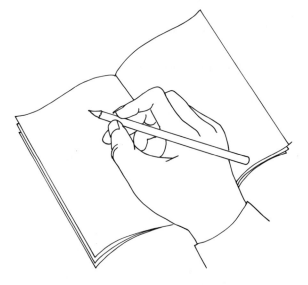

YOUR SIX-WEEK
SUCCESS JOURNAL

DAY 1/42

Physical Body (30–45 minutes)

Meditation (10–15 minutes)

Education (60 minutes)

Gratitude

1.

2.

3.

Action Steps
1.

2.

3.

Acknowledgement

DAY 2/42

Physical Body (30–45 minutes)

Meditation (10–15 minutes)

Education (60 minutes)

Gratitude

1.

2.

3.

Action Steps
1.

2.

3.

Acknowledgement

DAY 3/42

Physical Body (30–45 minutes)

Gratitude

1.

Meditation (10–15 minutes)

2.

Education (60 minutes)

3.

Action Steps
1.

2.

3.

Acknowledgement

DAY 4/42

Physical Body (30–45 minutes)

Meditation (10–15 minutes)

Education (60 minutes)

Gratitude

1.

2.

3.

Action Steps

1.

2.

3.

Acknowledgement

DAY 5/42

Physical Body (30–45 minutes)

Meditation (10–15 minutes)

Education (60 minutes)

Gratitude

1.

2.

3.

Action Steps

1.

2.

3.

Acknowledgement

DAY 6/42

Physical Body (30–45 minutes)

Meditation (10–15 minutes)

Education (60 minutes)

Gratitude

1.

2.

3.

Action Steps

1.

2.

3.

Acknowledgement

DAY 7/42

Physical Body (30–45 minutes)

Meditation (10–15 minutes)

Education (60 minutes)

Gratitude

1.

2.

3.

Action Steps
1.

2.

3.

Acknowledgement

DAY 8/42

Physical Body (30–45 minutes)

Gratitude

1.

Meditation (10–15 minutes)

2.

Education (60 minutes)

3.

Action Steps
1.

2.

3.

Acknowledgement

DAY 9/42

Physical Body (30–45 minutes)

Gratitude

1.

Meditation (10–15 minutes)

2.

Education (60 minutes)

3.

Action Steps
1.

2.

3.

Acknowledgement

DAY 10/42

Physical Body (30–45 minutes)

Meditation (10–15 minutes)

Education (60 minutes)

Gratitude

1.

2.

3.

Action Steps

1.

2.

3.

Acknowledgement

DAY 11/42

Physical Body (30–45 minutes)

Meditation (10–15 minutes)

Education (60 minutes)

Gratitude

1.

2.

3.

Action Steps

1.

2.

3.

Acknowledgement

DAY 12/42

Physical Body (30–45 minutes)

Meditation (10–15 minutes)

Education (60 minutes)

Gratitude

1.

2.

3.

Action Steps
1.

2.

3.

Acknowledgement

DAY 13/42

Physical Body (30–45 minutes)

Meditation (10–15 minutes)

Education (60 minutes)

Gratitude

1.

2.

3.

Action Steps
1.

2.

3.

Acknowledgement

DAY 14/42

Physical Body (30–45 minutes)

Gratitude

1.

Meditation (10–15 minutes)

2.

Education (60 minutes)

3.

Action Steps

1.

2.

3.

Acknowledgement

DAY 15/42

Physical Body (30–45 minutes)

Gratitude

1.

Meditation (10–15 minutes)

2.

Education (60 minutes)

3.

Action Steps
1.

2.

3.

Acknowledgement

DAY 16/42

Physical Body (30–45 minutes)

Meditation (10–15 minutes)

Education (60 minutes)

Gratitude

1.

2.

3.

Action Steps
1.

2.

3.

Acknowledgement

DAY 17/42

Physical Body (30–45 minutes)

Meditation (10–15 minutes)

Education (60 minutes)

Gratitude

1.

2.

3.

Action Steps
1.

2.

3.

Acknowledgement

DAY 18/42

Physical Body (30–45 minutes)

Gratitude

1.

Meditation (10–15 minutes)

2.

Education (60 minutes)

3.

Action Steps
1.

2.

3.

Acknowledgement

DAY 19/42

Physical Body (30–45 minutes)

Meditation (10–15 minutes)

Education (60 minutes)

Gratitude

1.

2.

3.

Action Steps
1.

2.

3.

Acknowledgement

DAY 20/42

Physical Body (30–45 minutes)

Gratitude

1.

Meditation (10–15 minutes)

2.

Education (60 minutes)

3.

Action Steps
1.

2.

3.

Acknowledgement

DAY 21/42

Physical Body (30–45 minutes)

Meditation (10–15 minutes)

Education (60 minutes)

Gratitude

1.

2.

3.

Action Steps
1.

2.

3.

Acknowledgement

DAY 22/42

Physical Body (30–45 minutes)

Gratitude

1.

Meditation (10–15 minutes)

2.

Education (60 minutes)

3.

Action Steps

1.

2.

3.

Acknowledgement

DAY 23/42

Physical Body (30–45 minutes)

Gratitude

1.

Meditation (10–15 minutes)

2.

Education (60 minutes)

3.

Action Steps
1.

2.

3.

Acknowledgement

DAY 24/42

Physical Body (30–45 minutes)

Meditation (10–15 minutes)

Education (60 minutes)

Gratitude

1.

2.

3.

Action Steps
1.

2.

3.

Acknowledgement

DAY 25/42

Physical Body (30–45 minutes)

Meditation (10–15 minutes)

Education (60 minutes)

Gratitude

1.

2.

3.

Action Steps
1.

2.

3.

Acknowledgement

DAY 26/42

Physical Body (30–45 minutes)

Meditation (10–15 minutes)

Education (60 minutes)

Gratitude

1.

2.

3.

Action Steps
1.

2.

3.

Acknowledgement

DAY 27/42

Physical Body (30–45 minutes)

Meditation (10–15 minutes)

Education (60 minutes)

Gratitude

1.

2.

3.

Action Steps
1.

2.

3.

Acknowledgement

DAY 28/42

Physical Body (30–45 minutes)

Gratitude

1.

Meditation (10–15 minutes)

2.

Education (60 minutes)

3.

Action Steps
1.

2.

3.

Acknowledgement

DAY 29/42

Physical Body (30–45 minutes)

Meditation (10–15 minutes)

Education (60 minutes)

Gratitude

1.

2.

3.

Action Steps
1.

2.

3.

Acknowledgement

DAY 30/42

Physical Body (30–45 minutes)

Meditation (10–15 minutes)

Education (60 minutes)

Gratitude

1.

2.

3.

Action Steps
1.

2.

3.

Acknowledgement

DAY 31/42

Physical Body (30–45 minutes)

Meditation (10–15 minutes)

Education (60 minutes)

Gratitude

1.

2.

3.

Action Steps

1.

2.

3.

Acknowledgement

DAY 32/42

Physical Body (30–45 minutes)

Meditation (10–15 minutes)

Education (60 minutes)

Gratitude

1.

2.

3.

Action Steps
1.

2.

3.

Acknowledgement

DAY 33/42

Physical Body (30–45 minutes)

Meditation (10–15 minutes)

Education (60 minutes)

Gratitude

1.

2.

3.

Action Steps
1.

2.

3.

Acknowledgement

DAY 34/42

Physical Body (30–45 minutes)

Meditation (10–15 minutes)

Education (60 minutes)

Gratitude

1.

2.

3.

Action Steps
1.

2.

3.

Acknowledgement

DAY 35/42

Physical Body (30–45 minutes)

Meditation (10–15 minutes)

Education (60 minutes)

Gratitude

1.

2.

3.

Action Steps
1.

2.

3.

Acknowledgement

DAY 36/42

Physical Body (30–45 minutes)

Meditation (10–15 minutes)

Education (60 minutes)

Gratitude

1.

2.

3.

Action Steps
1.

2.

3.

Acknowledgement

DAY 37/42

Physical Body (30–45 minutes)

Meditation (10–15 minutes)

Education (60 minutes)

Gratitude

1.

2.

3.

Action Steps

1.

2.

3.

Acknowledgement

DAY 38/42

Physical Body (30–45 minutes)

Gratitude

1.

Meditation (10–15 minutes)

2.

Education (60 minutes)

3.

Action Steps

1.

2.

3.

Acknowledgement

DAY 39/42

Physical Body (30–45 minutes)

Meditation (10–15 minutes)

Education (60 minutes)

Gratitude

1.

2.

3.

Action Steps
1.

2.

3.

Acknowledgement

DAY 40/42

Physical Body (30–45 minutes)

Meditation (10–15 minutes)

Education (60 minutes)

Gratitude

1.

2.

3.

Action Steps

1.

2.

3.

Acknowledgement

DAY 41/42

Physical Body (30–45 minutes)

Gratitude

1.

Meditation (10–15 minutes)

2.

Education (60 minutes)

3.

Action Steps
1.

2.

3.

Acknowledgement

DAY 42/42

Physical Body (30–45 minutes)

Meditation (10–15 minutes)

Education (60 minutes)

Gratitude

1.

2.

3.

Action Steps
1.

2.

3.

Acknowledgement

ABOUT THE AUTHOR

Pat Divilly is a bestselling author, motivational speaker and entrepreneur from the west coast of Ireland.

Pat's personal story has been told the world over, most noticeably by Facebook COO Sheryl Sandberg. He first became a household name when he went from being unemployed to establishing a phenomenally successful fitness business.

Pat's journey to success began back in 2011. After having failed in his first foray into personal training business, he moved back to Galway and started a small fitness class on his local beach. At the time, he had just five clients.

In little under four years, however, Pat's client base had reached over 10,000 through his gym classes and online training programmes.

With the belief that 'everyone can make a difference', Pat has used his public platform to help various organizations, and his fundraising efforts have resulted in over €250,000 being raised for charities throughout Ireland.

He now carries out personal development seminars and retreats around the world, helping people reach their full potential and achieve more fulfilment in their business and personal life.

Pat also runs a hugely successful podcast series which you can find on his website **www.patdivilly.com.**

ACKNOWLEDGEMENTS

Listing everyone I'd like to acknowledge would be a book in itself. I'm truly grateful for all the amazing people in my life. I'm blessed to have work that doesn't feel like work and countless 'clients' who have became great friends.

Though I can't mention everyone special thanks must go to:

Tara King. Thank you for helping me take all my ideas and structure them into this book. You're amazing at what you do!

Jenny and all the guys at Capstone/Wiley for helping make the book happen and allowing me this opportunity.

Rick and Janice Barrett for being a family of creative genies! Thank you for all the help.

Gill Carroll. My best buddy. Always there when I need support or guidance and always inspiring me with your leadership qualities and work ethic.

Thomas Palmer. It's been a hell of a journey thus far, brother! From classes in Ballybane to 24-hour mud runs in the desert to sold-out seminars. Thank you for everything.

Wayne Cantwell. From crazy nights out to quiet nights in! We're slowly growing up! I appreciate you being there for me every step of the way, especially during the struggles.

My staff and clients. Aoife, Elaine and Bernie – thank you guys for being a rock solid team committed to helping anyone who works with us. Thank you also to everyone who's bought a book, come to a seminar, trained at my gym or gone through an online programme. I appreciate you.

My teachers, mentors, podcast guests and mastermind partners. Dax Moy, Greg Muller, Dan Meredith, Justin Devonshire, Jamie Alderton, Stephen Somers, Yanik Silver and all the Maverick 1000 crew. Thank you all for inspiring me and helping me learn more about myself and the world.

Ken, Una, Danielle, Rona, Enda, Treasa, Marion, Claire, Daire, Chaz and Steve Deady. Unsung heroes that put in so much work on committees and charity events to make other people's lives easier. Thank you.

And finally my family – Mum, Dad, Áine, Colm and Liam – thank you, for everything.

INDEX